D0969745

BABY
NAMES

Town&Country

BABY NAMES

The Guide to Selecting The Perfect Name for Your Child

Foreword by Pamela Fiori

Introduction by Caroline Tiger

Illustrations by Tania Lee

HEARST BOOKS

A DIVISION OF STERLING PUBLISHING CO., INC.

NEW YORK

Copyright © 2004 by Hearst Communications, Inc.

Library of Congress Cataloging-in-Publication Data
Town & country baby names : the guide to selecting the perfect name
for your child / introduction by Caroline Tiger ; illustrated by Tania Lee.
    p. cm.
  Includes bibliographical references and index.
  ISBN 1-58816-408-X
 1. Names, Personal—Dictionaries.
CS2377.T69 2004
929.4'4'03—dc22

                     2004005220

10 9 8 7 6 5 4 3 2 1

Published by Hearst Books
A Division of Sterling Publishing Co., Inc.
387 Park Avenue South, New York, NY 10016

Town & Country is a trademark owned by Hearst Magazines Property,
Inc., in USA, and Hearst Communications, Inc., in Canada. Hearst
Books is a trademark owned by Hearst Communications, Inc.

www.townandcountrymag.com

Distributed in Canada by Sterling Publishing
$^{c}/_{o}$ Canadian Manda Group, 165 Dufferin Street
Toronto, Ontario, Canada M6K 3H6

Distributed in Australia by Capricorn Link (Australia) Pty. Ltd.
P.O. Box 704, Windsor, NSW 2756 Australia

Printed in China

ISBN 1-58816-408-X

No, Groucho is not my real name.
I'm breaking it in for a friend.
—*Groucho Marx*

∾

The name of a man is a numbing blow
from which he never recovers.
—*Marshall McLuhan*

CONTENTS

FOREWORD

I was born into an age when parents gave their children nice, simple names like Mary or Anne, John or William. Or else, they leaned on their heritage. So when my mother and father decided to call me Pamela, the rest of my family, mostly Italian-Americans, must have wondered what in the world was going on. "Pamela" was more appropriate for proper English girls. My relatives expected Angela or Maria.

Soon, more and more young girls—no matter what their backgrounds—were named Pamela and Leslie and Jennifer and Jessica. Meanwhile, the boys became Eric, Max, Sean and Jason. The Marys and Williams seemed to vanish, along with black-and-white TVs and manual typewriters.

Today, babies are being born to parents of nearly every age and almost every generation. Many are also adopted and hail from all over the planet. The choices of names are endless ... and therein lies the problem. What, for instance, possesses parents to give their newborn a highly unusual, attention-getting name? Don't they realize it could very well haunt that child for the rest of his or her life? Maybe it doesn't even occur to them, but it should.

I suppose there are justifications for certain names, but why call your daughter Apple, as one recent celebrity did? (And why not Tomato, Rhubarb or Sassafras?)

Then there are the couples who name their babies after someone currently in vogue: Britney or Brad, Paris or Beyonce. Imagine an annual board meeting, years from now, when shareholders ask the chairman of the company why she is known as L'il Kim.

There are all sorts of reasons for choosing certain names: a favorite flower (Rose, Iris, Violet, Lily); a coveted brand (Mercedes, Bentley, Tiffany, Hermes); an admired statesman (Lincoln, Jefferson, Winston); a legendary artist, author or character (Pablo, Frida, Leonardo, Shakespeare, Scarlett).

I am particularly intrigued by those who want to spell a perfectly common name differently (Aleeysha, Denys, Marq). And I am even more fascinated by those who insist on unconventional uses of upper and lower case: SallyJo, LeAnn, fitzPatrick, BillieBob. If you want your kid to stand out in a crowd, this is surely one way to do it. Of course, having a son or a daughter who is unique is what a great many parents wish for.

You see where this could lead. Hence, *Town & Country* offers this helpful little glossary of baby names. It is brimming with possibilities and may well inspire you to select the perfect appellation (Burgundy? Chardonnay?) for the little one. Read it carefully. Choose well. After all, it's not just a name, it's an identity. And it lasts no less than a lifetime.

—PAMELA FIORI, EDITOR IN CHIEF, *Town & Country*

INTRODUCTION

Which is more difficult—growing up as a boy named Sue, or as a boy named Courvoisier? We may have to wait until at least 2020 to find out. By then the seven boys born in 2000 called Courvoisier may be able to tell us about their lives with the name of a popular cognac. Of course, by 2020 the result will be moot. Parents will have moved on to the next trend—maybe it'll be naming their children after numbers like Four, Eighteen and Twenty-one; or herbs and spices like Cinnamon and Nutmeg. Naming children after alcoholic drinks is just the latest trend in baby-naming.

It wasn't always like this. In the 1580s half the boys in the Raleigh Colony, the first English settlement on American soil, were named John, Thomas or William. Fifty years later, in the 1630s, more than half the newborn girls in the Massachusetts Bay Colony received the name Mary, Elizabeth or Sarah. Parents in early America had it easy. They had far fewer options. It was their custom to christen their children with the name of a relative, of which there was a finite number. Nowadays, all bets are off. Surnames are given as first names, and parents are naming their children after places, products, movie characters and pop stars.

When did the madness begin? Researchers trace the growing diversity in baby naming to the 1960s, when the practice of giving family names began to subside. That's when names for girls began to stray from the norm. Names for boys stayed predictable until the 1980s, which was the real beginning of the boom in unusual baby names. Today, for the first time in history about half the baby boys born in America receive the top fifty most popular names. Less than half the baby girls have one of the top fifty names written on their birth certificates. More and more babies are named, well, uniquely.

Psychologists have all kinds of theories about the reason for the increase in popularity of Athena and the decrease in Jennifer. One researcher says it's a reaction to a society that's growing more generic. The more java we buy at Starbucks and armchairs we buy at Pottery Barn, the more we want to separate ourselves from our neighbors by distinguishing our children from the pack. On the other hand, perhaps trendy naming reflects our society's growing diversity of choices: We have hundreds of TV channels to choose from instead of the two networks that existed in the 1950s, and thanks to television, the Internet, foreign films and the ease with which we travel today, we're exposed to different countries and cultures—*and* different baby names.

Whatever the reason, we've been freed from John, Mary, Thomas and Elizabeth. But is it freedom—or is it tyranny? Having so many options can be terrifying. Imagine living in the 1950s, taking a time capsule to the year 2004, and walking into a supermarket to find that there are thirty-seven different types of cereal. How would you choose one? If this is your first baby, you may feel like that person from the 1950s standing perplexed in front of a sea of cereal boxes. If it's not your first, you'll be more familiar with the ins and outs of baby-naming, but chances are the game has changed since you named your last baby. Here are some tips to help you narrow the field.

Another Emily, Madison or Jacob?

Do some research to find out whether the name you're considering is popular. You may be taken by surprise, especially if this is your first child and you're unaware of recent naming trends. You may not want your daughter to be the tenth Emily in her pre-school class, destined to be known for the rest of her academic life as Emily L. The appendage of a last initial makes a person sound like one more cog in the machine. It may be reassuring at first to be one of many girls called Emily, but it will become irksome later on when your daughter is trying to forge her own identity. Check the Popular Baby Names page on the Social Security Administration's website (www.ssa.gov/OACT/babynames/) for a list of the most popular baby names by state. Poll other expectant mothers. Check chat rooms on websites where moms-to-be might be discussing their favorite baby names. If you are thinking of moving after your child is born, think about how unique your baby's name will be in your new hometown. A name that seems perfectly normal in an urban area may strike an awkward note in a rural region.

Do names have associations?

Common sense dictates that certain names come with stereotypes. Adolph is assumed a bully. So is Brutus. Bambi and Vanna are taken for intellectual lightweights. Jacqueline is elegant. But names, when attached to a real person or even to a photograph, transcend these stereotypes. Once someone meets your daughter, Bambi, who deftly quotes Shakespeare, that person's image of Bambi will change. Keep in mind, though, that first impressions can be formed before two people meet face-to-face. When Bambi sends in her application for a Ph.D. program, the person reviewing it may subconsciously handicap her chances.

The character traits we generally associate with peoples' names come from our collective impressions of public figures like politicians and entertainers, or characters in books, TV shows or movies (Adolph, Vanna, Buffy). But we also form impressions based on the individuals we run into during the course of our everyday lives. If someone was bullied by a Keith in seventh grade or mocked by a snob named Dawn in high school, those names may be ruined for that person forever. Obviously, you have no control over that when you're naming your baby.

There's also nothing you can do about the popular associations that might crop up during your child's lifetime. No method exists for predicting the names of the notorious criminals and infamous celebrities of the future. Think of all those named Ted Bundy out there who've been forced to use their middle names. Other coincidences are more fortunate—what man would object to being called James Dean?

What effect will that name have on your child?

Parents sometimes think they can alter a child's destiny by giving him or her the perfect name. If that's true, then it can also work the opposite way, right? Giving someone the wrong name can give him or her an imperfect destiny. Wrong. There's no definitive evidence that a name affects a child's level of popularity, mental health or achievement. It may have an indirect effect, since parents who give their child an unusual name are probably people who are individualists themselves. Their unconventional home will influence their child more than his name. Parents who prefer traditional names may be more inclined to follow convention, and their kids will be shaped more by this inclination than by being named John or Sarah.

In general, a name is an insignificant factor in a child's development, but there are exceptions. When children are given names with strong associations—and they don't share those associations—they might have a tough time. A skinny boy named Rocky, a Yo-Yo Ma with no musical talent or a Harmony with a short temper may have difficulty living up to the expectations implied by their names and are likely to be teased. And since it's impossible to tell a baby's personality or potential flaws in the first few hours after he's born, it may be safest to stick with a classic name.

The exception to *that* rule is the Junior issue. A son who inherits his dad's name may always feel as if he's number two, a lesser man, and that may affect his self-esteem. Particularly if Dad has a strong personality or achieves great success in life, his namesake will struggle, more so than an ordinary son, to live up to those expectations. Being known as "Little John" or "Johnny" or "Junior" for his entire adult life will only rub in that feeling of smallness. The third in a line has an even stronger mandate to uphold family expectations. This is why it might be better to give family names as middle names, or to skip a generation or two to repeat a first name. Besides, think of all the confusion you'll save when the phone rings for John.

Do you really want to saddle your child with a difficult, unwieldy name?

Remember, this is the first word she's going to learn how to spell, the first letters she'll have to learn how to form in big-block print. Why give her a doozie, especially if she already has a difficult surname? Make it easy on her. Don't give her a name that looks as if it's spelled wrong, the kind of name that she'll have to repeat over and over again when people pause and ask, "*How* do you spell that?" An unusual name may get your child noticed, but so will dressing him in a plaid jacket and paisley pants and sending him to school. Think about whether the attention he'll receive will be positive or negative. Often, it depends on the child. A confident one can carry an unusual name with aplomb. But how can you be sure he'll have the self-assurance to sport a name like Kugar?

When in doubt, subject your chosen name to the business-card test. Can you see the name printed on a cream-colored, embossed business card? Can you see your baby all grown up at a networking event, in a tailored Brooks Brothers suit, handing his business card to a colleague and *not* inducing a pause, or worse, snickers? Take it a step further. Give it the lawyer test. Can you see your baby all grown up, named Tallulah, and trying a criminal case before a judge and jury? Will she sound credible?

Also give your name the teasing test. Think of words that rhyme with it and be creative—Natalie Bratalie? Spell

out the initials to make sure they don't form an unfortu-
nate acronym, such as D.U.D. Another obstacle your
child might face is pronunciation. Is the name you're giving her likely to be mispronounced (such as "Lay" for
"Leigh")?

Good News for Boys

You may find it's easier to name a boy, because there are
fewer options. Girls have appropriated the unisex names
like Dylan, Casey, Morgan and Madison. That trend is
not new—Alice, Anne, Crystal, Lucy and Maud all used to
be boys' names. Once a name crosses the gender line into
the girls' club, it never goes back. Names cross more often
in that direction, since parents are more likely to stick
with traditional names for their sons and to experiment
with their daughters' names.

The fact that parents are giving their daughters
masculine-sounding names may indicate that they hope
their daughters will possess what are still seen in our
society as masculine traits, like ambition, athleticism and
assertiveness. There's also a rich tradition of strong
women with masculine names: Jo in *Little Women*; George
Eliot, the pseudonym of a female Victorian novelist; and
modern-day actresses such as Glenn Close, Sean Young
and Drew Barrymore.

∽

This book doesn't list every name that's ever been dreamed up. Courvoisier is not included. Instead, it includes names that we think will endure the test of time. Even if some of these names are currently out-of-fashion, we predict that they'll be back in the top ten or top fifty one day soon. We don't cover countless different spelling variations; in general, the traditional spelling is given along with the origin and meaning for each name. If you don't find anything that jumps out at you here, there are many other places to go for inspiration: your family tree, for instance. Look at a map of the country or consider names from countries from which your ancestors came. Who is your favorite fictional character? There are loads of great names thought up by imaginative novelists.

One last tip: however you do come to your decision, a child can always feel good about a name that has a satisfying story attached—something that goes beyond "We saw it in a magazine and thought it was nice." Even if she's the sixth Olivia in her third-grade class, she'll be the only Olivia whose parents met while they were in a production of *Twelfth Night* during summer stock, two years after college, and whose mom played the part of Olivia.

PART I

CLASSIC NAMES

Leave it to William and Sarah to ride out the waves of TV-inspired names and counterintuitive spellings. These are the kinds of names a baby can grow into and make her own. No rebelling against Cinderella by going punk-rock or goth; no futile attempts to live up to Elvis. After all, how many of us can live up to Elvis? A kid can work with Sarah or John. These names are like little black dresses— they let the wearer add the flash, or not.

∽

GIRLS' NAMES

· A ·

Abby
(Hebrew) a familiar
form of Abigail

Abigail
(Hebrew) father's joy

Acacia
(Greek) thorny

Ada
(Latin) helpful;
(German) a short form
of Adelaide

Adair
(Scottish) innovative

Addie
(Greek, German)
a familiar form of
Adelaide, Adrienne

Addison
(English) awesome

Adelaide
(German)
distinguished;
serene

Adeline
(English) a form
of Adelaide

Adelle
(German, English)
a short form of
Adelaide, Adeline

Adena
(Hebrew) precious

Adia
(African) God's gift

Adina
(Hebrew) high hopes

Adrienne
(Greek) rich;
(Latin) dark

Agatha
(Greek) kind hearted

Aggie
(Greek) a familiar
form of Agatha

Agnes
(Greek) pure

Aida
(Arabic) gift

Aidan
(Irish) fire

Aileen
(Scottish) light bearer

Ailey
(Irish) light and
friendly

Aimee
(Latin) an alternate
form of Amy;
(French) beloved

Ainsley
(Scottish) my own
meadow

Aisha
(Swahili) life, lively;
(Arabic) woman

Alana, Alanna
(Irish) attractive;
peaceful

Alanis
(French) shining star

Alba
(Latin) from Alba,
Italy, a city on
a white hill

Alberta
(French) noble and
bright; a feminine
form of Albert

Alessandra
(Italian) defender of
mankind

Alexandra
(Greek) defender
of mankind;
a feminine form
of Alexander

Alexandria
(Greek) an alternate
form of Alexandra

Alexis
(Greek) a short form
of Alexandra

Alfreda
(English) counsel from
the elves; a feminine
form of Alfred

Ali
(Greek) a familiar form
of Alice, Alicia
and Alison

Alice
(Greek) honest;
(German) noble

Alicia
(English) an alternate
form of Alice

Alison, Allison
(English) a form
of Alice

Alisa, Alissa
(Greek) an alternate
form of Alice

Allegra
(Latin) joyous

Allie
(Greek) a familiar
form of Alice

Alma
(Latin) good, soulful

Althea
(Greek) wholesome

Alva
(Spanish) fair, bright

Alyssa
(Greek) rational

"Must a name mean something?" Alice asked doubtfully.

"Of course it must," Humpty Dumpty said with a short laugh:

"My name means the shape I am—and a good handsome shape it is too. With a name like yours, you might be any shape, almost."

—from Alice's Adventures in Wonderland, by Lewis Carroll

Amanda
(Latin) much-loved

Amber
(French) amber

Amelia
(Latin) an alternate
form of Emily;
(German) industrious

Amelie
(German) a familiar
form of Amelia

Amy
(Latin) loved one

Anaïs
(French) a form
of Anne

Anastasia
(Greek) resurrection

Andrea
(Greek) strong,
courageous;
(Latin) the feminine
form of Andrew

Angela
(Greek) angel;
messenger

Angelica
(Greek) an alternate
form of Angela

Angelina
(Greek) a form of
Angela

Angie
(Greek) a familiar
form of Angela

Anita
(Spanish) a form
of Ann, Anna

Ann, Anne
(English) gracious

Anna
(Czech, Italian,
German, Swedish)
gracious

Anneliese
(Scandinavian)
gracious;
(German) religious

Annette
(French) a form
of Ann

Annie
(English) a familiar
form of Ann

Ansley
(English) happy
in the meadow

Antoinette
(French) a form
of Antonia

Antonia
(Greek) flourishing;
(Latin) praiseworthy;
a feminine form of
Anthony

April
(Latin) opening

Arabella
(Latin) beautiful altar

Arden
(English) valley
of the eagle

Aretha
(Greek) woman
of virtue

Ariel
(Hebrew) lioness
of God

Arielle
(French) a form
of Ariel

Arlene
(Irish) dedicated

Ashley
(English)
ash tree meadow

Astrid
(Scandinavian)
divine strength

Athena
(Greek) wise woman

Aubrey
(German) noble
being; (French)
blond leader

Audrey
(English) noble
strength

Augusta
(Latin) revered

Augustine
(Latin) majestic

Aurelia
(Latin) golden

Austin
(Latin) a short form of
Augustine

Ava
(Greek) an alternate
form of Eva

Avery
(French) flirtatious

Avis
(Latin) little bird

Ayla
(Hebrew)
strong as an oak

∽

· B ·

Babe
(Latin) a familiar form
of Barbara

Babette
(French) little Barbara

Babs
(Latin) a familiar form
of Barbara

Bailey
(English) bailiff

Bambi
(Italian) childlike,
baby girl

Barb
(Latin) a short form of
Barbara

Barbara
(Greek) foreign

Barrie
(Irish) markswoman;
a feminine form of
Barry

Bea, Bee
(American) short
forms of Beatrice

Beatrice
(Latin) blessed; happy;
bringer of joy

Bebe
(French) baby

Becky
(American) a familiar
form of Rebecca

Belinda
(Spanish) beautiful

Bella
(Latin) beautiful

Belle
(French) beautiful;
a short form of
Arabella, Belinda,
Isabel

Benecia
(Latin) a short fom
of Benedicta

Benedicta
(Latin) woman
blessed; a feminine
form of Benedict

Bernadette
(French) a form of
Bernadine

Bernadine
(German) brave as a
bear; (English) a
feminine form of
Bernard

Bernice
(Greek) bringer
of victory

Beryl
(Greek) sea green gem

Bess, Bessie
(Hebrew) familiar
forms of Elizabeth

Beth
(Hebrew, Aramaic)
house of God; a short
form of Bethany,
Elizabeth

Bethany
(Aramaic) house of figs

Betsy
(American) a familiar
form of Elizabeth

Bette
(French) a form
of Betty

Betty
(English) a familiar
form of Elizabeth

Bev
(English) a short
form of Beverly

Beverly
(English) beaver
stream; field

Bianca
(Italian) white

Bibi
(Latin) lively

Billie
(English)
strong-willed

Birdie
(English) bird

Blaine
(Irish) thin

Blair
(Scottish)
plains-dweller

Blaise
(French) one who
stammers

Blake
(English) dark

Blanche
(French) white,
pale

Blondie
(American) blond

Blythe
(English) carefree

Bobbi, Bobbie
(American) familiar
forms of Barbara,
Roberta

Bonnie, Bonny
(English, Scottish)
beautiful, pretty

Brandy
(Dutch) after-dinner
drink

Breana, Breanna
(Irish) alternate forms
of Briana

Breann, Breanne
(Irish) alternate forms
of Briana

Bree
(Irish) a short form
of Breann

Brenda
(Irish) little raven;
(English) sword

Brett
(Irish) a short form
of Britany

Briana, Brianna
(Irish) virtuous,
strong; feminine
forms of Brian

Brice
(English) quick

Bridey
(Irish) a familiar
form of Bridget

Bridget
(Irish) strong

**Bridgett,
Bridgette**
(Irish) alternate
forms of Bridget

Brionna
(Irish) happy

Britany, Brittany
(English) from Britain

Britney, Brittney
(English) alternate
forms of Britany,
Brittany

Bronwyn
(Welsh) white-breasted

Brooke
(English) brook,
stream; a feminine
form of Brook

Bryn, Brynn
(Latin) from the
boundary line;
(Welsh) mound

Bunny
(Greek) a familiar
form of Bernice;
(English) little rabbit

· C ·

Cady
(English) an alternate form of Kady

Caitlin
(Irish) pure; an alternate form of Cathleen

Caitlyn
(Irish) an alternate form of Caitlin

Cala, Calla
(Greek) beautiful

Callie
(Greek, Arabic) a familiar form of Cala, Callista

Callista
(Greek) most beautiful

Camellia
(Italian) evergreen or shrub

Cameron
(Scottish) crooked nose

Camilla
(Italian) Camille

Camille
(French) innocent

Candace
(Greek) glowing girl

Candy
(Greek) a familiar form of Candace

Cara
(Latin) dear one; (Irish) friend

Carey
(Welsh) a familiar
form of Cara,
Caroline, Karen,
Katherine

Carla
(Latin) an alternate
form of Carol, Caroline

Carlotta
(Italian) a form
of Charlotte

Carly
(English) a familiar
form of Caroline,
Charlotte

Carmel
(Hebrew) place name,
garden

Carmela,
Carmella
(Hebrew) garden;
vineyard

Carmen
(Latin) song

Carol
(English) strong
and womanly;
(French) joyful song;
(German) farmer

Carole
(English) an alternate
form of Carol

Carolina
(Italian) a form
of Caroline

Caroline
(French) petite
and womanly

Carolyn
(English) a form
of Caroline

Carrie
(English) a familiar
form of Carol,
Caroline

Casey
(Irish) brave

Cass
(Greek) a short form
of Cassandra

Cassandra
(Greek) helper of men

Cassia
(Greek) spicy
cinnamon

Cassidy
(Irish) clever girl

Cassie
(Greek) a familiar
form of Cassandra

Catherine
(Greek) pure;
(English) a form of
Katherine

Cathleen
(Irish) a form of
Catherine

Cathy
(Greek) a familiar
form of Catherine,
Cathleen

Cecilia
(Latin) blind, dim-
sighted; the sixth child

Celena
(Greek) an alternate
form of Selena

Celeste
(Latin) celestial,
heavenly

Celia
(Latin) a short form
of Cecilia

Celina
(Greek) an alternate
form of Celena

Celine
(Greek) an alternate
form of Celena

Cerise
(French) cherry red

Chandra
(Sanskrit) moon

Chantal
(French) singer
of songs

Charlene
(English) a form
of Caroline

Charlie
(German, English)
strong and womanly

Charlotte
(French) little woman;
a form of Caroline

Charmaine
(French) a form
of Carmen

Chelsea
(English) harbor

Cher
(French) beloved,
dearest

Cheri, Cherie
(French) familiar
forms of Cher

Cherish
(English) dearly held,
precious

Cherry
(French) cherry,
cherry red

Cheryl
(French) beloved

Chloe, Chlöe
(Greek) flowering

Chris
(Greek) a short form
of Christina

Chrissy
(English) a familiar
form of Christina

Christa
(German) a short form
of Christina

**Christian,
Christiana**
(Greek) alternate
forms of Christina

Christina
(Greek) Christian;
the anointed one

Christine
(French, English)
forms of Christina

Christy
(English) a short
form of Christina,
Christine

Cicely
(Latin) form of
Cecilia; clever

Cindy
(Greek) moon; (Latin)
a familiar form
of Cynthia

Claire
(French) a form
of Clara

Clara
(Latin) bright one

Clarice
(French) clear, bright

Clarissa
(Greek) smart and
clear-minded

Claudia
(Latin) lame;
a feminine form
of Claude

Claudette
(French) persevering

Clementine
(Latin) merciful;
a feminine form of
Clement

Cleo
(Greek) a short form
of Cleopatra

Cleopatra
(Greek) her
father's fame

Clio
(Greek) proclaimer;
glorifier

Codi, Cody
(English) soft-
hearted, pillow

Colby
(English) coal town

Colette
(Greek, French)
a familiar form
of Nicole

Colleen
(Irish) young girl

Connie
(Latin) a familiar form
of Constance

Constance
(Latin) loyal

Constantina
(Italian) loyal,
constant

Cora
(Greek) maiden

Coral
(Latin) coral

Cordelia
(Latin) warm-hearted
woman

Corina, Corinna
(Greek) familiar forms
of Corinne

Corinne
(Greek) maiden

Cornelia
(Latin) horn colored

Cosima
(Greek, German,
Italian) of the
universe; in harmony

Courtney
(English) from the
court

Crystal
(Latin) clear, brilliant
glass

Cynthia
(Greek, English)
moon goddess

∽

· D ·

Daisy
(English) day's eye

Dale
(English) valley

Dana
(English) from
Denmark;
bright as day

Danielle
(Hebrew, French)
God is my judge;
a feminine form
of Daniel

Daphne
(Greek) laurel tree

Dara
(Hebrew)
compassionate

Darby
(Irish) a free woman

Darci, Darcy
(Irish) dark

Darlene
(French) little darling

Daryl
(French) a short form
of Darlene

Dawn
(English) sunrise,
dawn

Debbie
(Hebrew) a short
form of Deborah

Deborah
(Hebrew) bee

Debra
(American) a short
form of Deborah

Dee
(Welsh) black, dark

Deirdre
(Irish) sorrowful;
wanderer

Delia
(Greek) visible;
from Delos

Delilah
(Hebrew) brooder

Della
(Greek) kind

Delphine
(Greek) from Delphi

Dena
(Hebrew) an alternate
form of Dinah

Denise
(French) wine-lover

Derry
(Irish) red-haired
woman

Desiree
(French) desired

Di
(Latin) a short form
of Diana, Diane

Diana, Dianna
(Latin) divine woman

Diane
(Latin) an alternate
form of Diana

Dina
(Hebrew) a short form
of Dinah

Dinah
(Hebrew) vindicated

Dionne
(Greek) divine queen

Dixie
(French) tenth

Dodie
(Greek) a familiar
form of Dorothy;
(Hebrew) beloved

Dolly
(American) a short
form of Dolores,
Dorothy

Dolores
(Spanish) woman of
sorrowful leaning

Dominique
(French) belonging
to God

Donatella
(Latin, Italian) gift

Donna
(Italian) ladylike
and genteel

Dora
(Greek) gift from God

Doreen
(Greek) an alternate
form of Dora; (Irish)
moody, sullen

Dori, Dory
(American) familiar
forms of Dora, Doria,
Doris, Dorothy

Doria
(Greek) from Doris,
Greece; a feminine
form of Dorian

Doris
(Greek) sea-loving,
sea nymph mother

Dory
(French) gilded,
gold hair

Dorothea
(Greek) an alternate
form of Dorothy

Dorothy
(Greek) God's gift

Dot
(Greek) a familiar
form of Dorothy

Dottie, Dotty
(Greek) familiar forms
of Dorothy

Drea
(American) adorable

Drew
(Greek) woman
of valor

Dylan
(Welsh) creative,
from the sea

∽

· E ·

Edie
(English) a familiar
form of Edith

Edith
(English) rich gift

Edna
(Hebrew) youthful

Edwina
(English) prosperous
friend; a feminine
form of Edwin

Effie
(Greek) of high morals

Eileen
(Irish) a form
of Helen

Elaine
(French) a form
of Helen

Elana
(Greek) a short
form of Eleanor

Eleanor
(Greek) light-hearted;
an alternate form
of Helen

Elena
(Greek) an alternate
form of Eleanor

Elisa
(Spanish, Italian,
English) a short form
of Elizabeth

Elise
(French, English)
a short form of
Elizabeth

Eliza
(Hebrew) a short form
of Elizabeth

Elizabeth
(Hebrew) consecrated
to God

Ella
(Greek) a short
form of Eleanor

Elle
(Scandinavian) woman

Ellen
(English) a form of
Eleanor, Helen

Ellie, Elly
(English) familiar
forms of Eleanor,
Ellen

Eloise
(German) high-spirited

Elsa
(Hebrew) a short form
of Elizabeth;
(German) noble

Elsie
(German) a familiar
form of Elsa

Emerald
(French) green
gemstone

Emily
(Latin) flatterer;
(German) industrious

Emma
(German) a short form
of Emily

Enid
(Welsh) lively

Erica, Erika
(Scandinavian) ruler
of others; (English)
brave ruler

Erin
(Irish) peace-making

Erma
(Latin) noble

Esmé
(French) a familiar
form of Esmeralda;
a form of Amy

Esmeralda
(Greek, Spanish)
a form of Emerald

Essie
(English) a short form
of Estelle, Esther

Estelle
(French) a form
of Esther

Esther
(Persian) shining star

Ethel
(English) noble

Etta
(German) little;
(English) short for
Henrietta

Eudora
(Greek) honored gift

Eugenia
(Greek) regal and
polished; a feminine
form of Eugene

Eunice
(Greek) joyful,
winning

Eva
(Hebrew) an alternate
form of Eve

Eve
(Hebrew) life

Evelyn
(English) hazelnut

· F ·

Faith
(English) faithful, fidelity

Fanny
(American) a familiar form of Frances

Farah, Farrah
(Arabic) joy

Fawn
(French) young deer

Faye
(English) an alternate form of Faith; (French) fairy, elf

Felicia
(Latin) joyful; fortunate

Felicity
(Latin) happy girl

Fern
(English) fern; (German) a short form of Fernanda

Fernanda
(German) bold, adventurous

Fifi
(French) jazzy

Fiona
(Irish) fair-haired

Flannery
(Irish) redhead

Flo
(American) a short form of Florence

Flora
(Latin) flower; a short form of Florence

Florence
(Latin) blooming,
flourishing

Flossie
(English) a familiar
form of Florence

Fran
(Latin) a short form
of Frances

Frances
(Latin) free;
of French origin

Francesca
(Italian) a form
of Frances

Francine
(French) a form
of Frances

Frankie
(American) a form
of Frances

Frannie, Franny
(English) familiar
forms of Frances

Freda, Freida, Frieda
(German) short forms
of Alfreda

Frederica
(German)
peacemaking

Freya
(Scandinavian)
goddess, beautiful

Frida
(Scandinavian) lovely

∾

· G ·

Gabriela, Gabriella
(Italian) alternate forms of Gabrielle

Gabrielle
(French) devoted to God; a feminine form of Gabriel

Gaby
(French) a familiar from of Gabrielle

Gail
(Hebrew) a short form of Abigail

Gay
(French) merry

Gayle
(English) an alternate form of Gail

Geena
(Italian) a form of Gina

Generosa
(Spanish) generous

Genevieve
(German, French) an alternate form of Guinevere

Georgeanne
(English) a combination of Georgia and Anne

Georgene
(English) a familiar form of Georgia

Georgette
(French) a form of Georgia

Georgia
(Greek) farmer;
a feminine form
of George

Georgianna
(English) combination
of Georgia and Anna,
bright-eyed

Georgina
(English) a form
of Georgia

Geraldine
(German) might with a
spear; a feminine form
of Gerald

Geri
(American) a familiar
form of Geraldine

Germaine
(French) from
Germany

Gertrude
(German) beloved
warrior

Gigi
(French) a familiar
form of Gilberte

Gilberte
(German) brilliant;
pledge; trustworthy

Gilda
(English) covered
with gold

Gillian
(Latin) an alternate
form of Jillian

Gina
(Italian) a short form
of Angelina, Eugenia,
Regina, Virginia

Ginger
(Latin) flower; spice;
a familiar form of
Virginia

Ginny
(English) a familiar
form of Ginger,
Virginia

Giselle
(German) pledge;
hostage

Gladys
(Latin) small sword;
(Irish) princess

Glenda
(Welsh) a form
of Glenna

Glenna
(Irish) valley, glen;
a feminine form of
Glenn

Gloria
(Latin) glorious

Glory
(Latin) an alternate
form of Gloria

Glynnis
(Irish) a narrow valley

Golda
(English) gold

Grace
(Latin) graceful

Greer
(Scottish) vigilant;
a feminine form
of Gregory

Greta
(German) a short form
of Gretchen, Margaret

Gretchen
(German) a form
of Margaret

Griselda
(German) gray woman
warrior

Guinevere
(French, Welsh) white
wave; white phantom

Gussie
(Latin) a short form
of Augusta

Gwen
(Welsh) a short form
of Guinevere,
Gwendolyn

Gwendolyn
(Welsh) white wave;
white browed;
new moon

Gwyneth
(Welsh) an alternate
form of Gwendolyn

~

· H ·

Hadassah
(Hebrew) myrtle tree

Hadley
(English) field
of heather

Hailey
(English) an alternate
form of Hayley

Haley
(Scandinavian)
heroine

Hallie
(Scandinavian) an
alternate form of Haley

Hana
(Japanese) flower;
(Slavic) a form of
Hannah

Hanna
(Hebrew) an alternate
form of Hannah

Hannah
(Hebrew) gracious

Happy
(English) cheerful,
happy

Harley
(English) the long
field

Harmony
(Latin) harmonious

Harriet
(French) ruler of
the household;
(English) an alternate
form of Henrietta

Hattie
(English) familiar
forms of Harriet,
Henrietta

Hayley
(English) hay meadow

Hazel
(English)
hazelnut tree

Heather
(English) flowering
heather

Heidi
(German) a short form
of Adelaide

Helaine
(Greek) a form of
Helen

Helen
(Greek) light

Helena
(Greek) an alternate
form of Helen

Helene
(French) a form of
Helen

Heloise
(German) renowned
in war

Henrietta
(English) ruler of the
household; a feminine
form of Henry

Hermione
(Greek) earthly

Hilary, Hillary
(Greek) cheerful, merry

Hollis
(English) near the
holly bushes

Holly
(English) holly tree

Honey
(Latin) a familiar form
of Honora;
(English) sweet

Honora
(Latin) honorable

Hope
(English) hope

Hortense
(Latin) gardener

∾

· I ·

Ida
(German)
hardworking;
(English) prosperous

Ilana
(Hebrew) tree

Iliana
(Greek) from Troy

Ima
(German) a familiar
form of Amelia

Imelda
(German) warrior

Imogen, Imogene
(Latin) image, likeness

Ina
(Greek) pure

Inez
(Latin) pure

Ingrid
(Scandinavian)
hero's daughter;
beautiful daughter

Iphigenia
(Greek) sacrifice

Irene
(Greek) peaceful

Iris
(Greek) rainbow

Irma
(Latin) an alternate
form of Erma

**Isabel, Isabelle,
Isabella**
(Spanish) consecrated
to God; a form of
Elizabeth

Isadora
(Latin) gift of Isis

Isolde
(Welsh) fair lady

Ivana
(Slavic)
God is gracious

Ivory
(Latin) made of ivory

Ivy
(English) ivy tree

∾

· J ·

Jacki, Jackie
(American) familiar
forms of Jacqueline

Jacklyn
(American) a short
form of Jacqueline

Jaclyn
(American) a short
form of Jacqueline

Jacqueline
(French) supplanter,
substitute; little
Jacqui; a feminine
form of Jacques

Jacqui
(French) a short form
of Jacqueline

Jade
(Spanish) jade

Jaime, Jaimee
(French) I love

Jami, Jamie
(Hebrew) supplanter;
(English) feminine
forms of James

Jan
(English) a short form
of Jane, Janet, Janice

Jana
(Slavic) a form of Jane

Jane
(Hebrew) God is
gracious; a feminine
form of John

Janelle
(French) a form
of Jane

Janet
(English) a form
of Jane

Janice
(Hebrew)
God is gracious

Janie
(English) a familiar
form of Jane

Janine
(French) a form
of Jane

Janis
(English) a form
of Jane

Janna
(Hebrew) a short
form of Johana

Jasmine
(Persian) jasmine
flower

Jayne
(English) a form
of Jane

Jean, Jeanne
(Scottish) God is
gracious; forms
of Jane, Joan

Jeanette
(French) a form
of Jean

Jeanie
(Scottish) a familiar
form of Jean

Jeanine, Jenine
(Scottish) alternate
forms of Jean

Jena, Jenna
(Arabic) small bird;
(Welsh) a short form
of Jennifer

Jenni, Jennie, Jenny
(Welsh) familiar forms
of Jennifer

Jennifer
(Welsh) white wave;
an alternate form of
Guinevere

Jeri, Jerri, Jerrie
(American) alternate
forms of Geri

Jessica
(Hebrew) wealthy;
a feminine form
of Jesse

Jessie
(Hebrew) a short form
of Jessica

Jewel
(French) precious gem

Jill
(English) a short form
of Jillian

Jillian
(Latin) youthful

Jo
(American) a short
form of Joanna,
Josephine

Joan
(Hebrew) God is
gracious; an alternate
form of Jane

Joanie
(Hebrew) a familiar
form of Joan

Joanna
(English) a form
of Joan

Jocelyn
(Latin) joyous

Jodi, Jodie, Jody
(American) familiar
forms of Judith

Joelle
(Hebrew)
God is willing

Johana
(Hebrew) the Lord is
gracious

Jolie
(French) pretty

Joni
(American) a familiar
form of Joan

Jordan
(Hebrew) descending

Josephine
(French) God will
increase; a feminine
form of Joseph

Josie
(Hebrew) a familiar
form of Josephine

Joy
(Latin) joyous

Joyce
(Latin) joyous

Juanita
(Spanish) a form
of Jane, Joan

Judith
(Hebrew) praised

Judy
(Hebrew) a familiar
form of Judith

Julia
(Latin) youthful;
a feminine form
of Julius

Juliana, Julianna
(Czech, Spanish,
Hungarian) forms
of Julia

Julie
(English) a form
of Julia

Juliet, Juliette
(French) forms
of Julia

June
(Latin) born in
the sixth month

Justina
(Italian) a form
of Justine

Justine
(Latin) just,
righteous; a feminine
form of Justin

∾

· K ·

Kady
(English) an alternate
form of Katy

Kaitlin, Kaitlyn
(Irish) pure;
an alternate form
of Caitlin

Kara
(Greek, Danish) pure;
an alternate form of
Katherine

Karen
(Greek) pure;
an alternate form
of Katherine

Kari
(Greek) pure

Karin
(Scandinavian)
a form of Karen

Kate
(Greek) pure;
(English) a short form
of Katherine

Katharine
(Greek) an alternate
form of Katherine

Katherine
(Greek) pure

Kathi, Kathy
(English) familiar
forms of Katherine,
Kathleen

Kathleen
(Irish) a form
of Katherine

Kathryn
(English) a form of
Katherine

Katie
(English) a familiar
form of Kate

Katrina
(German) a form of
Katherine

Katy
(English) a familiar
form of Kate

Kay
(Greek) rejoicer;
(Latin) merry; a short
form of Katherine

Keeley, Keely
(Irish) alternate forms
of Kelly

Kelley
(Irish) an alternate
form of Kelly

Kelli, Kellie
(Irish) familiar forms
of Kelly

Kelly
(Irish) brave warrior

Kelsey
(Scandinavian,
Scottish) ship island

Kenda
(English) water baby

Kendall
(English) ruler of
the valley

Kendra
(English) an alternate
form of Kenda

Kerri, Kerrie
(Irish) alternate forms
of Kerry

Kerry
(Irish) dark haired

Kim
(Vietnamese) needle;
(English) a short form
of Kimberly

Kimberlee,
Kimberley
(English) alternate
forms of Kimberly

Kimberly
(English) chief ruler

Kirsta
(Scandinavian) an
alternate form of
Kirsten

Kirsten
(Greek) Christian,
anointed;
(Scandinavian) a form
of Christine

Kirstin
(Scandinavian)
an alternate form
of Kirsten

Kirsty
(Scandinavian)
a familiar form
of Kirsten

Kitty
(Greek) a familiar
form of Katherine

Kris
(American) a short
form of Kristine; an
alternate form of
Chris

Krissy
(American) a familiar
form of Kris

Krista
(Czech) a form of
Christina

Kristen
(Greek) Christian,
anointed;
(Scandinavian) a form
of Christine

Kristi, Kristie
(Scandinavian) short
forms of Kristine

Kristin
(Scandinavian) an
alternate form of
Kristen

Kristina
(Greek) Christian,
anointed;
(Scandinavian) a form
of Christina

Kristine
(Scandinavian) a form
of Christine

Kristy
(American) a familiar
form of Kristine

Kyle
(Irish) attractive

Kylie
(West Australian
Aboriginal) curled
stick, boomerang;
(Irish) a familiar form
of Kyle

Kyra
(Greek) ladylike

· L ·

Lacey, Lacy
(Greek) a familiar
form of Larissa;
(Latin) cheerful

Laci, Lacie
(Latin) alternate
forms of Lacey

Laine
(French) a short form
of Elaine

Lana
(Latin) wooly;
(Irish) attractive,
peaceful

Lane
(English) narrow road

Lara
(Greek) cheerful;
(Latin) shining,
famous

Larissa
(Greek) cheerful

Lark
(English) skylark

Laura
(Latin) crowned with
laurel; a feminine
form of Laurence

Laurel
(Latin) laurel tree

Lauren
(English) a form
of Laura

Laurie
(English) a familiar
form of Laura

Laverne
(Latin) springtime

Lea
(Hawaiian) in
Hawaiian mythology,
the goddess of canoe
makers

Leah
(Hebrew) weary

Leanna
(English) an alternate
form of Liana

Lee
(Chinese) plum;
(Irish) poetic;
(English) meadow

Leeann, Leeanne
(English)
a combination of
Lee and Ann

Leigh
(English) an alternate
form of Lee

Leila
(Hebrew) dark beauty,
night; (Arabic) born
at night

Lelia
(Greek) fair speech

Lena
(Greek) a short form
of Eleanor; (Hebrew)
dwelling or lodging

Leona
(German)
brave as a lioness

Lesley
(Scottish) gray fortress

Leslie
(Scottish) an alternate
form of Lesley

Leticia
(Latin) joy

Letty
(English) a familiar
form of Leticia

Lexi
(Greek) a familiar
form of Alexandra

Libby
(Hebrew) a familiar
form of Elizabeth

Liana
(French) bound,
wrapped up;
(Latin) youth

Lidia
(Greek) an alternate
form of Lydia

Lila
(Arabic) night

Lilith
(Arabic) of the night;
night demon

Lillian
(Latin) lily flower

Lily
(Latin, Arabic)
a familiar form of
Lilith, Lillian

Lina
(Greek) light;
(Latin) an alternate
form of Lena

Linda
(Spanish) pretty

Lindsay
(English) an alternate
form of Lindsey

Lindsey
(English) linden tree
island

Linette
(Welsh) idol;
(French) bird

Lisa
(Hebrew) consecrated
to God; (English) a
short form of
Elizabeth

Lisette
(French) a form
of Lisa

Liv
(Latin) a short form
of Livia, Olivia

Livia
(Hebrew) crown;
a familiar form of
Olivia; (Latin) olive

Liz
(English) a short form
of Elizabeth

Liza
(American) a short
form of Elizabeth

Lizzy
(American) a familiar
form of Elizabeth

Lois
(German) famous
warrior; an alternate
form of Louise

Lola
(Spanish) a familiar
form of Carlotta,
Dolores, Louise

Lolita
(Spanish) sorrowful;
a familiar form of Lola

Loren
(American)
an alternate form
of Lauren

Lorena
(English) an alternate
form of Lauren, Loren

Loretta
(English) a familiar
form of Laura

Lori
(Latin) crowned with
laurel; (American) a
familiar form of Laura

Lorraine
(Latin) sorrowful;
(French) from
Lorraine, a region
in France

Lou
(American) a short
form of Louise, Luella

Louisa
(English) a familiar
form of Louise

Louise
(German) famous
warrior; a feminine
form of Louis

Luann
(Hebrew, German)
graceful woman
warrior

Lucia
(Italian, Spanish)
a form of Lucy

Lucie
(French) a familiar
form of Lucy

Lucille
(English) a familiar
form of Lucy

Lucinda
(Latin) a familiar form
of Lucy

Lucretia
(Latin) rich, rewarded

Lucy

(Latin) light, bringer
of light; a feminine
form of Lucius

Luella

(German) a familiar
form of Louise

Lulu

(Arabic) pearl

Lydia

(Greek) from Lydia,
an ancient land once
ruled by King Midas

Lynette

(Welsh) idol; (French)
a form of Lynn

Lynn, Lynne

(English) waterfall;
pool below a waterfall

· M ·

Mabel
(Latin) lovable

Mackenzie
(Irish) daughter of
the wise leader

Maddie
(English) a familiar
form of Madeline

Madeleine
(French) a form
of Madeline

Madeline
(Greek) high tower;
(English) from
Magdala, England;
an alternate form
of Magdalen

Madge
(Greek) a familiar
form of Madeline,
Margaret

Madison
(English) good;
son of Maud

Mae
(English) an alternate
form of May

Maeve
(Irish) joyous

Magdalen
(Greek) high tower

Maggie
(Greek) pearl;
(English) a familiar
form of Magdalen,
Margaret

Magnolia
(Latin) flowering tree

Mallorie
(French) an alternate
form of Mallory

Mallory
(German) army
counselor;
(French) unlucky

Mandy
(Latin) lovable;
a familiar form of
Amanda, Melinda

Marcella
(Latin) martial,
warlike; a feminine
form of Marcellus

Marci, Marcie
(English) familiar
forms of Marcella,
Marcia

Marcia
(Latin) martial,
warlike; an alternate
form of Marcella

Marcy
(English) an alternate
form of Marci

Margaret
(Greek) pearl

Margarita
(Italian, Spanish)
a form of Margaret

Marge
(English) a short form
of Margaret, Marjorie

Margie
(English) a familiar
form of Marge,
Margaret

Margo, Margot
(French) forms of
Margaret

Marguerite
(French) a form
of Margaret

Maria
(Hebrew) bitter;
sea of bitterness;
(Italian, Spanish)
a form of Mary

Mariah
(Hebrew) an alternate
form of Mary

Marian
(English) an alternate
form of Maryann

Mariana
(Spanish) a form
of Marian

Marie
(French) a form of
Mary

Mariel
(German, Dutch)
a form of Mary

Marigold
(English) a plant with
yellow or orange
flowers

Marilyn
(Hebrew) Mary's line
of descendents

Marina
(Latin) sea

Marion
(French) a form
of Mary

Maris
(Latin) sea

Marisa
(Latin) sea

Marissa
(Latin) an alternate
form of Maris, Marisa

Marjorie
(Greek) a familiar
form of Margaret

Marla
(English) a short form
of Marlena, Marlene

Marlena
(German) a form of
Marlene

Marlene
(Greek) high tower;
(Slavic) a form of
Magdalen

Marsha
(English) a form
of Marcia

Marta
(English) a short form
of Martha, Martina

Martha
(Aramaic) lady;
sorrowful

Martina
(Latin) martial,
warlike; a feminine
form of Martin

Mary
(Hebrew) bitter; sea of
bitterness

Maryann, Maryanne
(English)
combinations of
Mary and Ann

Matilda
(German)
powerful battler

Mattie, Matty
(English) familiar
forms of Martha,
Matilda

Queen Mary, wife of George V, had eight names, more than any other queen: Victoria Mary Augusta Louisa Olga Pauline Claudine Agnes. The next most name-laden queen was Alexandra, consort of King Edward VII, with six names: Alexandra Caroline Mary Charlotte Louisa Julia.

∽

Maud, Maude
(English) short forms
of Madeline, Matilda

Maura
(Irish) dark

Maureen
(French) dark; (Irish)
a form of Mary

Mauve
(French) violet
colored

Mavis
(French) song bird

Maxine
(Latin) greatest;
a feminine form
of Maximilian

May
(Latin) great;
(English) flower;
month of May

Maya
(Hindi) God's creative
power; (Greek) mother;
grandmother;
(Latin) great

Meagan
(Irish) an alternate
form of Megan

Meaghan
(Welsh) a form
of Megan

Meg
(English) a familiar
form of Margaret,
Megan

Megan
(Greek) pearl; great;
(Irish) a form
of Margaret

Meghan
(Welsh) a form
of Megan

Mel
(Portuguese, Spanish)
sweet as honey

Melanie
(Greek) dark skinned

Melba
(Greek) soft; slender;
(Latin) mallow flower

Melinda
(Greek) honey

Melissa
(Greek) honey bee

Melly
(American) a familiar
form of names
beginning with "Mel"

Melonie
(American) an
alternate form of
Melanie

Melody
(Greek) song, melody

Mercedes
(Latin) reward,
payment; (Spanish)
merciful

Mercy
(English)
compassionate,
merciful

Meredith
(Welsh) protector
of the sea

Merry
(English) cheerful,
happy

Meryl
(German) famous;
(Irish) shining sea

Mia
(Italian) mine

Michaela
(Hebrew) who is like
the Lord?; a feminine
form of Michael

Michele
(Italian) a form
of Michaela

Michelle
(French) who is like
the Lord?; a form of
Michaela

Mikaela
(Hebrew) an alternate
form of Michaela

Mila
(Italian, Slavic) a short
form of Camilla

Mildred
(English) gentle
counselor

Millicent
(Greek) an alternate
form of Melissa;
(English) industrious

Millie, Milly
(English) familiar
forms of Amelia,
Camille, Emily,
Melissa, Mildred,
Millicent

Mina
(German) love

Mindy
(Greek) a familiar
form of Melinda

Minnie
(American) a familiar
form of Mina

Miranda
(Latin) strange;
wonderful; admirable

Miriam
(Hebrew) bitter,
sea of bitterness

Missy
(English) a familiar
form of Melissa,
Millicent

Misty
(English) shrouded
by mist

Molly
(Irish) a familiar
form of Mary

Mona
(Greek) a short form
of Monica, Ramona

Monica
(Greek) solitary;
(Latin) advisor

Monika
(German) a form
of Monica

Monique
(French) a form
of Monica

Morgan
(Welsh) seashore

Muriel
(Irish) shining sea;
a form of Mary

Mykaela
(American) a form
of Mikaela

Myra
(Latin) fragrant
ointment; a feminine
form of Myron

Myrna
(Irish) beloved

Myrtle
(Greek) dark green
shrub

· N ·

Nadia
(French, Slavic)
hopeful

Nadine
(French, Slavic)
an alternate form
of Nadia

Nan
(German) a short form
of Fernanda;
(English) an alternate
form of Ann

Nancy
(English) gracious

Nanette
(French) giving,
gracious

Naomi
(Hebrew) pleasant,
beautiful

Nastasia
(Greek) an alternate
form of Anastasia

Natalia
(Russian) a form
of Natalie

Natalie
(Latin) born of
Christmas day

Natasha
(Russian) a form
of Natalie

Neely
(Irish) sparking smile

Nellie
(English) a familiar
form of Cornelia,
Eleanor, Helen

Nettie
(French) a familiar
form of Annette,
Antoinette

Nicki
(French) a familiar
form of Nicole

Nicola
(Italian) a form
of Nicole

Nicole
(French) victorious
people; a feminine
form of Nicholas

Nicolette
(French) an alternate
form of Nicole

Nina
(Hebrew) a familiar
form of Hannah

Noël
(Latin) Christmas

Noelle
(French) Christmas;
a form of Noel

Nola
(Latin) small bell;
(Irish) famous; noble

Nora
(Greek) light

Noreen
(Irish) a form of
Eleanor, Nora

Norma
(Latin) rule, precept

∽

· O ·

Octavia
(Latin) eighth

Odelia
(Greek) ode; melodic

Odessa
(Greek) odyssey,
long voyage

Odetta
(German, French)
a form of Odelia

Olga
(Russian) holy

Olive
(Latin) olive tree

Olivia
(Latin) olive tree

Olympia
(Greek) heavenly

Oona
(Latin) unity

Opal
(Hindi) precious stone

Ophelia
(Greek) helper

· P ·

Page
(French) young
assistant

Paige
(English) young child

Paloma
(Spanish) dove

Pamela
(Greek) honey

Pansy
(Greek) flower;
flagrant

Pat
(Latin) a short form
of Patricia, Patsy

Patience
(English) patient

Patricia
(Latin) noblewoman;
a feminine form of
Patrick

Patsy
(Latin) a familiar form
of Patricia

Patty
(English) a familiar
form of Patricia

Paula
(Latin) small;
a feminine form of Paul

Paulette
(French) a familiar
form of Paula

Pauline
(Latin) a familiar form
of Paula

Pearl
(Latin) jewel

Peggy
(Greek) a familiar
form of Margaret

Penelope
(Greek) weaver

Penny
(Greek) a familiar
form of Penelope

Perri
(Greek, Latin) small
rock; a feminine form
of Perry

Persephone
(Greek) springtime

Phillippa
(Greek) lover of
horses; a feminine
form of Phillip

Philomena
(Greek) love song;
loved one

Phoebe
(Greek) shining

Phyllis
(Greek) green bough

Pia
(Italian) devout

Polly
(Latin) a familiar
form of Paula

Portia
(Latin) offering

Priscilla
(Latin) ancient

Prudence
(Latin) cautious;
discreet

∾

· Q ·

Queenie
(English) queen

Quinby
(Scandinavian)
queen's estate

Quincy
(Irish) fifth

Quinn
(German, English)
queen

Quintana
(Latin) fifth;
a feminine form
of Quentin

∾

· R ·

Rachel, Rachael
(Hebrew)
a female sheep

Rachelle
(French) a form
of Rachel

Racquel
(French) a form
of Rachel

Rae
(English) doe;
(Hebrew) a short form
of Rachel

Ramona
(Spanish) mighty;
wise protector

Randall
(English) protected

Randi, Randy
(English) familiar
forms of Miranda,
Randall

Raphaela
(Hebrew) healed
by God

Raquel
(French) a form
of Rachel

Rea
(Greek) earth

Reba
(Hebrew) fourth-born

Rebecca
(Hebrew) tied, bound

Regan
(Irish) child of
the ruler

Regina
(Latin) queen;
(English) king's
advisor; a feminine
form of Reginald

Rena
(Hebrew) song; joy

Renata
(French) an alternate
form of Renée

Rene
(Greek) a short form
of Irene, Renée

Renée
(French) born again

Rhea
(Greek) earth

Rhoda
(Greek) from Rhodes

Rhonda
(Welsh) grand

Ricki, Rikki
(American) familiar
forms of Erica,
Frederica

Riley
(Irish) valiant

Rita
(Greek) a short form
of Margarita

Roberta
(English) famous
brilliance; a feminine
form of Robert

Robin
(English) robin

Robyn
(English) an alternate
form of Robin

Rochelle
(French) little rock

Ronni, Ronnie
(English) feminine
forms of Ronald

Rori, Rory
(Irish) famous
brilliance; famous
ruler

Ros, Roz
(English) short forms
of Rosalind, Rosalyn

Rosa
(Italian, Spanish)
a form of Rose

Rosalie
(English) a form
of Rosalind

Rosalind
(Spanish) fair rose

Rosalyn
(Spanish) an alternate
form of Rosalind

Rosamond
(German) famous
guardian

**Rosanna,
Roseanna**
(English)
combinations
of Rose and Anna

**Rosanne,
Roseanne**
(English)
combinations
of Rose and Anne

Rosario
(Filipino, Spanish)
rosary

Rose
(Latin) rose

Rosemarie
(English)
a combination
of Rose and Marie

Rosemary
(English)
a combination
of Rose and Mary

Rosie
(English) a familiar
form of Rosalind,
Rosanna, Rose

Rowena
(Welsh) fair-haired;
(English) famous
friend

Roxana, Roxanna
(Persian) alternate
forms of Roxann,
Roxanne

Roxann, Roxanne
(Persian) sunrise

Roxy
(Persian) a familiar
form of Roxann

Ruby
(French)
precious stone

Ruth
(Hebrew) friendship

Ruthie
(Hebrew) a familiar
form of Ruth

· S ·

Sabrina
(Latin) boundary line

Sadie
(Hebrew) a familiar
form of Sarah

Sage
(English) wise

Sally
(English) princess;
a familiar form of Sarah

Samantha
(Aramaic) listener;
(Hebrew) told by God

Sandi
(Greek) a familiar
form of Sandra

Sandra
(Greek) defender
of mankind

Sandy
(Greek) a familiar
form of Cassandra,
Sandra

Sara
(Hebrew) an alternate
form of Sarah

Sarah
(Hebrew) princess

Sasha
(Russian) defender
of mankind

Savannah
(Spanish) treeless
plain

Scarlett
(English) bright red

Schuyler
(Dutch) a form
of Skyler

Sebastiane
(Greek) venerable;
(Latin) revered;
(French) a feminine
form of Sebastian

Selena
(Greek) moon

Selina
(Greek) an alternate
form of Celina, Selena

Selma
(German) divine
protector; (Irish) fair,
just; a feminine form
of Anselm

Serafina
(Hebrew) burning;
ardent

Serena
(Latin) peaceful

Shae
(Irish) an alternate
form of Shea

Shana
(Hebrew)
God is gracious;
(Irish)
a form of Jane

Shane
(Irish) an alternate
form of Shana

Shanna
(Irish) an alternate
form of Shana,
Shannon

Shannon
(Irish) small and wise

Shari
(French) beloved,
dearest; an alternate
form of Cheri

Sharon
(Hebrew) desert plain

Shauna
(Irish) an alternate
form of Shana

Shea
(Irish) fairy palace

Sheila
(Latin) blind;
(Irish) a form
of Cecilia

Shelby
(English) ledge estate

Shelley, Shelly
(English) meadow
on the ledge

Sheri, Sherri
(French) alternate
forms of Sherry

Sherry
(French) beloved,
dearest; a familiar
form of Sheryl

Sheryl
(French) beloved;
an alternate form
of Cheryl

Shirley
(English) bright
meadow

Shona
(Irish) a form of Jane

Shoshana
(Hebrew) lily

Sierra
(Irish) black;
(Spanish) saw toothed

Sigourney
(English) victorious
conqueror

Sigrid
(Scandinavian)
victorious counselor

Silvia
(Latin) an alternate
form of Sylvia

Simone
(Hebrew) she heard;
(French) a feminine
form of Simon

Skye
(Arabic) water giver;
(Dutch) a short form
of Skyler

Skyler
(Dutch) sheltering

Sofia
(Greek) an alternate
form of Sophia

Solange
(French) dignified

Sondra
(Greek) defender
of mankind

Sonia
(Russian, Slavic)
an alternate form
of Sonya

Sonja
(Scandinavian)
a form of Sonya

Sonya
(Greek) wise;
(Russian, Slavic)
a form of Sophia

Sophia
(Greek) wise

Sophie
(Greek) a familiar
form of Sophia

Stacey, Stacy
(Greek) resurrection

Staci
(Greek) an alternate
form of Stacey

Stefanie
(Greek) an alternate
form of Stephanie

Steffi
(Greek) a familiar
form of Stefanie,
Stephanie

Stella
(Latin) star; (French)
a familiar form of
Estelle

Stephanie
(Greek) crowned;
a feminine form of
Stephan

Stevie
(Greek) a familiar
form of Stephanie

Stockard
(English) stockyard

Sue
(Hebrew) a short form
of Susan, Susanna

Summer
(English) summertime

Sunny
(English) bright,
cheerful

Susan
(Hebrew) lily

Susanna,
Susannah
(Hebrew) alternate
forms of Susan

Susie
(American) a familiar
form of Susan,
Susanna

Suzanne
(English) a form of
Susan

Suzette
(French) a form of
Susan

Svetlana
(Russian) bright light

Sybil
(Greek) prophet

Sydney
(French) from Saint
Denis, France; a
feminine form of
Sidney

Sylvia
(Latin) forest

∾

· T ·

Tabatha
(Greek, Aramaic) an
alternate form of
Tabitha

Tabby
(English) a familiar
form of Tabitha

Tabitha
(Greek, Aramaic)
gazelle

Taffy
(Welsh) beloved

Talia
(Greek) blooming;
(Hebrew) dew from
heaven; a short form
of Natalie

Tallulah
(Choctaw) leaping
water

Tamara
(Hebrew) palm tree

Tammi, Tammie
(English) alternate
forms of Tammy

Tammy
(Hebrew) a familiar
form of Tamara;
(English) twin

Tandy
(English) team

Tania
(Russian, Slavic)
fairy queen

Tansy
(Greek) immortal;
(Latin) tenacious,
persistent

Tanya
(Russian, Slavic) fairy
queen; a short form of
Tatiana

Tara
(Aramaic) throw;
carry; (Irish) rocky hill

Tari
(Irish) a familiar
form of Tara

Taryn
(Irish) an alternate
form of Tara

Tasha
(Greek) born of
Christmas day;
(Russian) a short form
of Natasha

Tate
(English) a short form
of Tatum

Tatiana
(Slavic) fairy queen

Tatum
(English) cheerful

Taylor
(English) tailor

Teresa,
(Greek) reaper;
an alternate form
of Theresa

Teri, Terri, Terry
(Greek) a familiar
form of Theresa

Tess, Tessa
(Greek) a short form
of Theresa

Tessie
(Greek) a familiar
form of Theresa

Thalia
(Greek) an alternate
form of Talia

Thea
(Greek) goddess;
a short form of Althea

Thelma
(Greek) willful

Theodora
(Greek) gift of God;
a feminine form of
Theodore

Theresa
(Greek) reaper

Therese
(Greek) an alternate
form of Theresa

Thora
(Scandinavian)
thunder; a feminine
form of Thor

Tia
(Greek) princess

Tiffani, Tiffanie
(Latin) alternate
forms of Tiffany

Tiffany
(Greek) trinity

Tiffy
(Latin) a familiar
form of Tiffany

Tilda
(German) a short
form of Matilda

Tillie
(German) a familiar
form of Matilda

Tina
(Spanish, American)
a short form of
Augustine, Martina,
Christina

Tish
(Latin) an alternate
form of Tisha

Tisha
(Latin) joy; a short
form of Leticia

Titania
(Greek) giant

Tobi, Toby
(Hebrew) God is good;
a feminine form of
Tobias

Tonia
(Latin, Slavic) an
alternate form of
Toni, Tonya

Tonya
(Slavic) fairy queen

Topsy
(English) on top

Tori
(Japanese) bird;
(English) an alternate
form of Tory

Tracey, Tracy
(Greek) a familiar
form of Theresa;
(Latin) warrior

Traci, Tracie
(Latin) alternate
forms of Tracey

Tricia
(Latin) an alternate
form of Trisha

Trish
(Latin) a short from of
Beatrice, Trisha

Trisha
(Latin) noblewoman;
a familiar form of
Patricia

Trista
(Latin) a short form
of Tristen

Tristen
(Latin) bold;
a feminine form
of Tristan

Trixie
(American) a familiar
form of Beatrice

Trudy
(German) a familiar
form of Gertrude

Twyla
(English) woven of
double thread

Tyler
(English) tailor

Tyne
(English) river

Tyra
(Scandinavian) battler

∾

· U ·

Ula
(Basque) the Virgin
Mary; (Irish) sea jewel

Ulla
(Latin) a short form of
Ursula; (German,
Swedish) willful

Uma
(Hindi) mother

Una
(Latin) one; united;
(Irish) a form of
Agnes

Ursula
(Greek) little bear

∾

· V ·

Val
(Latin) a short form
of Valentina, Valerie

Valentina
(Latin) strong

Valerie
(Latin) strong

Vanessa
(Greek) butterfly

Vanity
(English) vain

Vanna
(Greek) a short form
of Vanessa

Venus
(Latin) love

Vera
(Latin) true; a short
form of Veronica

Verity
(Latin) truthful

Veronica
(Latin) true image

Veronique,
Véronique
(French) forms
of Veronica

Vicki
(Latin) a familiar form
of Victoria

Vicky
(Latin) a familiar form
of Victoria

Victoria
(Latin) victorious

Viola
(Latin) violet; stringed
instrument in the
violin family

Violet
(French) a plant with
purplish blue flowers

Virginia
(Latin) pure, virginal

Vita
(Latin) life

Viv
(Latin) a short form
of Vivian

Vivian
(Latin) full of life

∾

· W ·

Wallis
(English) from Wales;
a feminine form of
Wallace

Wanda
(German) wanderer

Wendi
(Welsh) an alternate
form of Wendy

Wendy
(Welsh) white; light
skinned; a familiar form
of Gwendolyn, Wanda

Whitney
(English) white island

Wilhelmina
(German) determined
guardian; a feminine
form of Wilhelm,
William

Willa
(German) a short form
of Wilhelmina

Wilma
(German) a short form
of Wilhelmina

Win
(German) a short form
of Winifred

Winifred
(Welsh) an alternate
form of Guinevere

Winnie
(English) a familiar
form of Edwina,
Gwyneth, Winnifred,
Winona, Wynne

Winona
(Lakota) oldest
daughter

Wren
(English) wren,
songbird

Wynne
(Welsh) white, light
skinned; a short form
of Guinivere, Gwyneth

∾

· X ·

Xandra
(Greek) an alternate
form of Zandra;
(Spanish) a short form
of Alexandra

Xaviera
(Basque) owner of the
new house; a feminine
form of Xavier

Xena
(Greek) girl from afar

∾

· Y ·

Yasmin, Yasmine
(Persian) alternate
forms of Jasmine

Yoko
(Japanese) good girl

Yolanda
(Greek) violet flower

Yvette
(French) a familiar
form of Yvonne

Yvonne
(French) young archer

· Z ·

Zandra
(Greek) an alternate
form of Sandra

Zara
(Hebrew) an alternate
form of Sarah, Zora

Zelda
(German) a short form
of Griselda

Zena
(Greek) welcoming

Zoe, Zoë
(Greek) life

Zondra
(Greek) an alternate
form of Zandra

Zora
(Slavic) aurora; dawn

BOYS' NAMES

· A ·

Aaron
(Hebrew) enlightened

Abbott
(Hebrew) father, abbot

Abe
(Hebrew) a short form
of Abel, Abraham

Abel
(Hebrew) breath

Abraham
(Hebrew) father
of many

Abram
(Hebrew) a short form
of Abraham

Adair
(Scottish) oak-tree
ford

Adam
(Hebrew) earth;
son of the red earth

Addison
(English) son of Adam

Adlai
(Hebrew) my
ornament

Adrian
(Latin) from Adria,
a north Italian city

Adrien
(French) a form
of Adrian

Aidan
(Irish) fire

Ainsley
(Scottish) his very
own meadow

Al
(Irish) a short form of
Alan, Albert, Alexander

Alan
(Irish) handsome;
peaceful

Alastair
(Scottish) a form of
Alexander

Alban
(Latin) from Alba,
Italy, a city on
a white hill

Albert
(English) noble
and bright

Alby
(German, French)
familiar forms of
Albert

Alcott
(English) old cottage

Alden
(English) old;
wise protector

Aldrich
(English) wise
counselor

Alec
(Greek) a short form
of Alexander

Alex
(Greek) a short form
of Alexander

Alexander
(Greek) defender
of mankind

Alexis
(Greek) a short form
of Alexander

Alfie
(English) a familiar
form of Alfred

Alfred
(English) counsel
from the elves; wise
counselor

Alfredo
(Italian, Spanish)
a form of Alfred

Alger
(English) a short form
of Algernon

Algernon
(English) bearded,
wearing a moustache

Ali
(Arabic) exalted one

Allan, Allen
(Irish) alternate forms
of Alan

Alton
(English) old town

Alvin
(Latin) white;
light skinned

Amadeus
(Latin) loves God

Ambrose
(Greek) immortal

Ames
(French) friend

Amory
(German) an alternate
form of Emory

Amos
(Hebrew) borne,
carried

Anatole
(Greek) from the east

Anders
(Swedish) a form
of Andrew

André
(French) a form
of Andrew

Andreas
(Greek) an alternate
form of Andrew

Andrew
(Greek) strong, manly,
courageous

Andy
(Greek) a short form
of Andrew

Angus
(Scottish) exceptional,
outstanding

Ansel
(French) follower
of a nobleman

Anselm
(German) divine
protector

Ansley
(Scottish) an alternate
form of Ainsley

Anson
(German) divine;
(English) Anne's son

Anthony
(Latin) praiseworthy;
(Greek) flourishing

Antoine
(French) a form
of Anthony

Anton
(Slavic) a form
of Anthony

Antonio
(Italian) a form
of Anthony

Antony
(Latin) an alternate
form of Anthony

Archer
(English) bowman

Archibald
(German) bold

Argus
(Danish) watchful,
vigilant

Ari
(Greek) a short form
of Aristotle;
(Hebrew) a short form
of Ariel

Ariel
(Hebrew) lion of God

Arion
(Greek) enchanted

Aristotle
(Greek) best; wise

Arledge
(English) lake with
the hares

Arlen
(Irish) pledge

Arlo
(English) fortified hill

Armand
(Latin) noble

Armstrong
(English) strong arm

Arnie
(German) a familiar
form of Arnold

Arnold
(German) eagle ruler

Art
(English) a short form
of Arthur

Arthur
(Irish) noble; lofty
hill; (Scottish) bear;
(English) rock

Artie
(English) a familiar
form of Arthur

Asa
(Hebrew) physician,
healer

Ascot
(English) eastern
cottage; style of
necktie

Ash
(Hebrew) ash tree

Ashby
(Hebrew) an alternate
form of Ash

Asher
(Hebrew) happy;
blessed

Ashford
(English) ash-tree
ford

Ashley
(English) ash-tree
meadow

Ashton
(English) ash-tree
settlement

Atherton
(English) town by
a spring

Atlas
(Greek) lifted; carried

Atwood
(English) at the forest

Aubrey
(German) noble;
bear-like

Auden
(English) old friend

Audie
(English) a familiar
form of Edward

Augie
(Latin) a familiar form
of August

August
(Latin) a short form of
Augustine, Augustus

Augustine
(Latin) majestic

Augustus
(Latin) majestic;
venerable

Austin
(Latin) a short form
of Augustine

Averill
(French) born in April

Avery
(English) a form
of Aubrey

Avi
(Hebrew)
God is my father

Avram
(Hebrew) an alternate
form of Abraham,
Abram

Axel
(Latin) axe; (German)
small oak tree; source
of life

Ayers
(English) heir to a
fortune

∾

· B ·

Bailey
(French) bailiff,
steward

Bainbridge
(Irish) fair bridge

Baker
(English) baker

Baldwin
(German) bold friend

Bancroft
(English) bean field

Barclay
(Scottish, English)
birch tree meadow

Barry
(Welsh) son of Harry;
(Irish) spear;
marksman

Bart
(Hebrew) a short form
of Bartholomew

Bartholomew
(Hebrew) farmer's son

Barton
(English) barley farm;
Bart's town

Baxter
(English) an alternate
form of Baker

Beau
(French) handsome

Beaufort
(French) beautiful fort

Beaumont
(French) beautiful
mountain

Beauregard
(French) handsome;
beautiful gaze

Ben
(Hebrew) a short form
of Benjamin

Benedict
(Latin) blessed

Benjamin
(Hebrew) son of my
right hand

Bennett
(Latin) little
blessed one

Benny
(Hebrew) a familiar
form of Benjamin

Benson
(Hebrew) son of Ben

Bentley
(English) moor;
coarse grass meadow

Benton
(English) Ben's town;
town on the moors

Bernard
(German) brave as
a bear

Bernie
(German) a familiar
form of Bernard

Bertrand
(German) bright
shield

Bill
(German) a short
form of William

Billy
(German) a familiar
form of Bill, William

Blaine
(Irish) thin, lean;
(English) river source

Blair
(Irish) plain, field

Blake
(English) attractive;
dark

Bo
(English) a form
of Beau

Bob
(English) a short from
of Robert

Boris
(Slavic) battler,
warrior

Boyd
(Scottish) blond

Brad
(English) a short form
of Bradford, Bradley

Bradford
(English) broad river

Bradley
(English) broad
meadow

Brady
(Irish) spirited;
(English) broad island

Brandon
(English) beacon hill

Branson
(English) son of
Brandon

Brendan
(Irish) little raven

Brenden
(Irish) an alternate
form of Brendan

Brennan, Brennen
(English, Irish)
alternate forms of
Brendan

Brent
(English) a short form
of Brenton

Brenton
(English) steep hill

Bret, Brett
(Scottish)
man from Britain

Brewster
(English) brewer

Brian
(Irish, Scottish)
strong; virtuous;
honorable

Brice
(Welsh) alert;
ambitious

Brigham
(English) covered
bridge

Broderick
(Welsh) son of the
famous ruler;
(English) broad ridge

Brody
(Irish) ditch;
canal builder

Brook
(English) brook,
stream

Brooks
(English) son of Brook

Bruce
(French) brushwood
thicket, woods

Bruno
(English) brown-
skinned

Bryan
(Irish) strong;
virtuous; honorable;
an alternate form
of Brian

Bryant
(Irish) an alternate
form of Bryan

Bryce
(Welsh) an alternate
form of Brice

Bryon
(German) cottage;
(English) bear

Buck
(English) male deer

Buckley
(English) meadow of
the deer

Bud
(English) herald,
messenger

Burt
(English) a short form
of Burton

Burton
(English) fortified
town

Byron
(French) cottage;
(English) barn

· C ·

Cain
(Hebrew) spear,
gatherer

Caleb
(Hebrew) dog,
faithful;
(Arabic) bold, brave

Calvin
(Latin) bald

Cameron
(Scottish)
crooked nose

Campbell
(Latin, French)
beautiful field;
(Scottish) crooked
mouth

Carl
(German) farmer;
(English) strong and
manly

Carlisle
(English) Carl's island

Carmine
(Latin) song

Carter
(English) one who
drives carts

Carver
(English) one who
carves wood

Casey
(Irish) brave

Cash
(Latin) vain

Casper
(Persian) he who
guards the treasure

Cassidy
(Irish) ingenious,
clever

Cecil
(Latin) blind one

Cedric
(English) battle
chieftain

Chad
(English) warrior

Chadwick
(English)
warrior's town

Chaim
(Hebrew) life

Chance
(English) good
fortune; a short form
of Chancellor

Chancellor
(English)
record-keeper

Chandler
(English) candle-maker

Channing
(French) official
of the church

Charles
(German) farmer;
(English) strong
and manly

Chase
(French) hunter

Chester
(English) a short form
of Rochester

Chet
(English) a short form
of Chester

Chip
(English) a familiar
form of Charles

Chris
(Greek) a short form
of Christian,
Christopher

Christian
(Greek) follower
of Christ, anointed

Christopher
(Greek) Christ-bearer

Chuck
(American) a familiar
form of Charles

Churchill
(English) church on
the hill

Clancy
(Irish) redheaded
fighter

Clarence
(Latin) clear,
victorious

Clark
(French) cleric,
scholar

Claude
(Latin, French) lame

Clay
(English) clay pit

Clayton
(English) town built
on clay

Clement
(Latin) merciful

Cliff
(English) a short form
of Clifford, Clifton

Clifford
(English) cliff at the
river crossing

Clifton
(English) cliff town

Clint
(English) a short form
of Clinton

Clinton
(English) hill town

Clive
(English) an alternate
form of Cliff

Clyde
(Welsh) warm

Cody
(English) cushion

Colby
(English) dark,
dark-haired

Cole
(Greek) a short form
of Nicholas;
(Latin) cabbage farmer;
(English) a short form
of Coleman

Coleman
(Latin) cabbage farmer;
(English) coal miner

Colin
(Greek) a short form
of Nicholas;
(Irish) young cub

Collin
(Scottish) a form of
Colin, Collins

Collins
(Greek) son of Colin;
(Irish) holly

Colt
(English) young horse,
frisky; a short form of
Colter, Colton

Colter
(English) herd of colts

Colton
(English) coal town

Connor
(Scottish) wise

Conrad
(German) brave
counselor

Conroy
(Irish) wise

Constantine
(Latin) firm, constant

Cooper
(English) barrel maker

Cornelius
(Greek) cornel tree;
(Latin) horn colored

Craig
(Irish, Scottish) crag,
steep rock

Curt
(Latin) a short form
of Curtis

Curtis
(Latin) enclosure;
(French) courteous

Cy
(Persian) a short
form of Cyrus

Cyril
(Greek) lordly

Cyrus
(Persian) sun

༄

· D ·

Dale
(English) dale, valley

Dalton
(English) town in the
valley

Damian
(Greek) tamer, soother

Dan
(Hebrew) a short form
of Daniel

Daniel
(Hebrew) God is my
judge

Danny
(Hebrew) a familiar
form of Daniel

Darby
(Irish) free;
(English) deer park

Darcy
(Irish) dark;
(French) from Arcy

Darrell
(French) darling,
beloved; grove of
oak trees

Darren
(Irish) great;
(English) small, rocky
hill

Darryl
(French) darling,
beloved

Daryl
(French) an alternate
form of Darryl

Dashiell
(French) page boy

Dave
(Hebrew) a short
form of David

Davey
(Hebrew) a familiar
form of David

David
(Hebrew) beloved

Davis
(Welsh) son of David

Dean
(French) leader;
(English) valley

Delaney
(Irish) descendant of
the challenge

Dempsey
(Irish) proud

Denis
(Greek) an alternate
form of Dennis

Dennis
(Greek) from
mythology: a follower
of Dionysius, the god
of wine

Denny
(Greek) a familiar
form of Dennis

Dennison
(English) son
of Dennis

Derek
(German) ruler of
the people

Desmond
(Irish) from south
Munster

Dewey
(Welsh) prized

DeWitt
(Flemish) blond

Dexter
(Latin) dexterous,
adroit; (English)
fabric dyer

Dick
(German) a short form
of Frederick, Richard

Diego
(Spanish) a form
of Jacob, James

Digby
(Irish) ditch town

Dillon
(Irish) loyal, faithful

Dino
(German) little sword;
(Italian) a form
of Dean

Dirk
(German) a short form
of Derek

**Dominic,
Dominick**
(Latin) belonging
to the Lord

Don
(Scottish) a short form
of Donald

Donald
(Scottish) world
leader; proud ruler

Donovan
(Irish) dark warrior

Dorian
(Greek) from Doris,
Greece

Doug
(Scottish) a short form
of Dougal, Douglas

Douglas
(Scottish) dark river,
dark stream

Dov
(Hebrew) a familiar
form of David

Drake
(English) dragon

Drew
(Welsh) wise;
(English) a short form
of Andrew

Duane
(Irish) an alternate
form of Dwayne

Duncan
(Scottish)
brown warrior

Dunstan
(English) brownstone
fortress

Dustin
(English)
brown rock quarry

Dwayne
(Irish) dark

Dwight
(English) a form
of DeWitt

Dylan
(Welsh) sea

· E ·

Earl
(Irish) pledge;
(English) nobleman

Ed
(English) a short form
of Edgar, Edward

Eddie, Eddy
(English) familiar
forms of Edgar,
Edward

Edgar
(English) successful
spearman

Edmond
(English) an alternate
form of Edmund

Edmund
(English) prosperous
protector

Edward
(English) prosperous
guardian

Edwin
(English) prosperous
friend

Eli
(Hebrew) uplifted;
a short form of Elijah,

Elias
(Greek) a form
of Elijah

Elijah
(Hebrew) the Lord
is my God

Ellery
(Hebrew)
elder tree island

Elliot, Elliott
(English) forms
of Eli, Elijah

Ellis
(English) a form
of Elias

Ellison
(English) son of Ellis

Elton
(English) old town

Emerson
(German, English)
son of Emery

Emery
(German) industrious
leader

**Emmanuel,
Emanuel**
(Hebrew)
God is with us

Emmett
(German) industrious,
strong

Emory
(German) an alternate
form of Emery

Eric
(German) a short
form of Frederick;
(Scandinavian) ruler
of all; (English)
brave ruler

Erich
(Czech, German)
a form of Eric

Erik
(Scandinavian)
an alternate form
of Eric

Erin
(Irish) peaceful

Ernest
(English) earnest,
sincere

Ernie
(English) a familiar
form of Ernest

Ethan
(Hebrew) strong, firm

Eugene
(Greek) born
to nobility

Evan
(Irish) young warrior

Everett
(English) boar
hardness

Ezekiel
(Hebrew) strength
of God

Ezra
(Hebrew)
helper, strong

∾

· F ·

Fairfax
(English) blond

Felix
(Latin) fortunate,
happy

Ferdinand
(German) daring,
adventurous

Fielding
(English) field,
field worker

Finn
(Irish) blond haired,
light skinned

Finnegan
(Irish) light skinned,
white

Fitz
(English) son

Fitzgerald
(English)
son of Gerald

Fitzroy
(Irish) son of Roy

Fitzhugh
(English) son of Hugh

Fitzpatrick
(English)
son of Patrick

Fletcher
(English) arrow
featherer, arrow maker

Floyd
(English) a form
of Lloyd

Flynn
(Irish) son of
the red-haired man

Forrest
(French) forest,
woodsman

Francis
(Latin) free;
from France

Frank
(English) a short form
of Francis, Franklin

Frankie
(English) a familiar
form of Frank

Franklin
(English) free
landowner

Fraser
(French) strawberry;
(English) curly-haired

Fred
(German) a short form
of Frederick

Freddie
(German) a familiar
form of Frederick

Frederick
(German)
peaceful ruler

೧୨

· G ·

Gabriel
(Hebrew) devoted
to God

Gallagher
(Irish) eager helper

Gardner
(English) gardener

Gareth
(Welsh) gentle

Garrett
(Irish) brave spearman

Garth
(Scandinavian)
garden, gardener

Gary
(German) mighty
spearman;
(English) a familiar
form of Gerald

Gene
(Greek) well born;
a short form of Eugene

Geoff
(English) a short form
of Geoffrey

Geoffrey
(English) divinely
peaceful; a form
of Jeffrey

George
(Greek) farmer

Gerald
(German) mighty
spearman

Gerard
(English) brave
spearman

Gerry
(English) a familiar
form of Gerald

Gideon
(Hebrew) tree cutter

Gifford
(English) bold giver

Gilbert
(English) brilliant
pledge; trustworthy

Glen, Glenn
(Irish) short forms
of Glendon

Glendon
(Scottish) fortress
in the glen

Godfrey
(German) a form of
Jeffrey;
(Irish) God's peace

Gordon
(English)
triangular hill

Grady
(Irish) noble;
illustrious

Graham
(English) grand home

Granger
(French) farmer

Grant
(English) a short form
of Grantland

Grantland
(English) great plains

Granville
(French) large village

Gray
(English) gray haired

Graydon
(English) gray hill

Grayson
(English) bailiff's son

Greg, Gregg
(Latin) short forms
of Gregory

Gregory
(Latin) vigilant
watchman

Griffin
(Latin) hooked nose

Griffith
(Welsh) fierce chief,
ruddy

Gus
(Scandinavian) a short
form of Gustave

Gustave
(Scandinavian)
staff of the Goths

Guy
(Hebrew) valley;
(German) warrior;
(French) guide

~

· H ·

Hadley
(English) heather-
covered meadow

Hal
(English) a short form
of Hall, Harold

Haley
(Irish) ingenious

Hall
(English) manor, hall

Hamilton
(English) proud estate

Hank
(American) a familiar
form of Henry

Hans
(Scandinavian)
a form of John

Harold
(Scandinavian)
army ruler

Harper
(English) harp player

Harris
(English) a short form
of Harrison

Harrison
(English) son of Harry

Harry
(English) a familiar
form of Harold

Hart
(English) a short form
of Hartley

Hartley
(English) deer meadow

Harvey
(German) army warrior

Haywood
(English) hedged forest

Hector
(Greek) steadfast

Henderson
(Scottish, English) son of Henry

Henry
(German) ruler of the household

Herb
(German) a short form of Herbert

Herbert
(German) glorious soldier

Herman
(Latin) noble

Holt
(English) forest

Homer
(Greek) hostage; pledge; security

Horace
(Latin) keeper of the hours

Howard
(English) watchman

Howell
(Welsh) remarkable

Howie
(English) a familiar form of Howard

Hoyt
(Irish) mind; spirit

Hubert
(German) bright
mind, bright spirit

Hugh
(English) a short form
of Hubert

Hugo
(Latin) a form
of Hugh

Humphrey
(German) peaceful
strength

Hunter
(English) hunter

∾

• I •

Ian
(Scottish) a form
of John

Ike
(Hebrew) a familiar
form of Isaac

Immanuel
(Hebrew) an alternate
form of Emmanuel

Ira
(Hebrew) watchful

Irv
(Irish, Welsh, English)
a short form of Irvin

Irvin
(Irish, Welsh, English)
a short form of Irving

Irving
(Irish) handsome;
(Welsh) white river;
(English) sea friend

Irwin
(English) an alternate
form of Irving

Isaac
(Hebrew) laughter

Isaiah
(Hebrew) God is
my salvation

Ishmael
(Hebrew) the Lord
will hear

Ivan
(Russian) a form
of John

∾

· J ·

Jack
(American) a familiar
form of Jacob, John

Jackson
(English) son of Jack

Jacob
(Hebrew) supplanter,
substitute

Jacques
(French) a form
of Jacob, James

Jaime
(Spanish) a form
of Jacob, James

Jake
(Hebrew) a short
form of Jacob

James
(Hebrew) supplanter,
substitute; (English) a
form of Jacob

Jameson
(English) son of James

Jamie
(English) a familiar
form of James

Jan
(Dutch, Slavic)
a form of John

Jared
(Hebrew) descendant

Jason
(Greek) healer

Jasper
(English) a form
of Casper

Jay
(English) a short form
of James, Jason

Jeff
(English) a short form
of Jefferson, Jeffrey

Jefferson
(English) son of Jeff

Jeffery
(English) an alternate
form of Jeffrey

Jeffrey
(English) divinely
peaceful

Jeremiah
(Hebrew)
God will uplift

Jeremy
(English) a form
of Jeremiah

Jerome
(Latin) holy

Jerry
(English) a familiar
form of Gerald,
Gerard

Jesse, Jessie
(Hebrew) wealthy

Jim
(English) a short
form of James

Jimmie, Jimmy
(English) familiar
forms of Jim

Joe
(Hebrew) a short form
of Joseph

Joel
(Hebrew)
God is willing

Joey
(Hebrew) a familiar
form of Joe, Joseph

John
(Hebrew)
God is gracious

Johnathan
(Hebrew) an alternate
form of Jonathan

Johnathon
(Hebrew) an alternate
form of Jonathon

Johnny
(Hebrew) a familiar
form of John

Jon
(Hebrew) an alternate
form of John; a short
form of Jonathan

Jonah
(Hebrew) dove

Jonas
(Hebrew)
he accomplishes

Jonathan
(Hebrew) gift of God

Jonathon
(Hebrew) an alternate
form of Jonathan

Jordan
(Hebrew) descending

José
(Spanish)
a form of Joseph

Joseph
(Hebrew) God will add

Josh
(Hebrew) a short form
of Joshua

Joshua
(Hebrew)
God is my salvation

Juan
(Spanish)
a form of John

Judah
(Hebrew) praised

Judd
(Hebrew)
a short form of Judah

Jude
(Latin) a short form
of Judah

Judson
(English) son of Judd

Julian
(Greek, Latin)
an alternate form
of Julius

Julien
(Latin) an alternate
form of Julian

Julius
(Greek, Latin)
youthful, downy
bearded

Justin
(Latin) just, righteous

∾

The name John derives from the Hebrew Johanan, meaning "God is gracious." John was not a common English name until the eleventh century. The Norman conquerors brought it to Great Britain in various forms including the old French "Jehan." Jehan became anglicized into John. There are more than 100 variations of the name John in over thirty different languages, including Evan, Giovanni, Hans, Ian, Ivan, Jan, Jean, Jock, Johannes, Jon, Jonas, Jonathan, Juan, Owen, Sean, and Zane.

· K ·

Karl
(German) an alternate
form of Carl

Keith
(Welsh) forest;
(Scottish) battle place

Kelly
(Irish) warrior

Kelsey
(Scandinavian)
island of ships

Kelvin
(Irish, English)
narrow river

Ken
(Scottish) a short form
of Kendall, Kendrick,
Kenneth

Kendall
(English) valley
of the river Kent

Kendrick
(Scottish) royal
chieftain

Kennedy
(Irish) helmeted chief

Kenneth
(Irish) handsome;
(English) royal oath

Kent
(Welsh) white, bright;
(English) a short form
of Kenton

Kenton
(English) from Kent,
England

Kenyon
(Irish) white haired,
blond

Kerry
(Irish) dark,
dark haired

Kevin
(Irish) handsome

Kim
(English) a short form
of Kimball

Kimball
(Greek) hollow vessel;
(English) warrior chief

Kip, Kipp
(English) pointed hill

Kirby
(English) cottage
by the water

Kirk
(Scandinavian) church

Kurt
(Latin, German,
French) courteous;
enclosure

Kurtis
(Latin, French) an
alternate form of
Curtis

Kyle
(Irish) narrow piece of
land, place where
cattle graze

∾

· L ·

Lance
(German) a short form
of Lancelot

Lancelot
(French) attendant

Lane
(English) narrow road

Langston
(English) long,
narrow town

Larry
(Latin) a familiar form
of Lawrence

Laurence
(Latin) crowned
with laurel

Lawrence
(Latin) an alternate
form of Laurence

Lee
(English) a short form
of names containing
"lee"

Leigh
(English) an alternate
form of Lee

Lenny
(German) a familiar
form of Leonard

Leo
(Latin) lion

Leon
(Greek, German)
a short form
of Leonard

Leonard
(German)
brave as a lion

Leroy
(French) king

Les
(Scottish, English)
a short form of Leslie,
Lester

Lesley
(Scottish) gray fortress

Leslie
(Scottish) an alternate
form of Lesley

Lester
(English) from
Leicester, England

Levi
(Hebrew)
joined in harmony

Lew
(English) a short form
of Lewis

Lewis
(English) a form
of Louis

Lex
(English) a short form
of Alexander

Liam
(Irish) a form
of William

Lincoln
(English) town
by the pool

Lindley
(English) linden field

Lindsay
(English) an alternate
form of Lindsey

Lindsey
(English) linden-tree
island

Linus
(Greek) flaxen haired

Lionel
(French) lion cub

Lloyd
(Welsh) gray haired,
holy

Lorne
(Latin) a short form
of Lawrence

Lou
(German) a short form
of Louis

Louie
(German) a familiar
form of Louis

Louis
(German) famous
warrior

Lucas
(German, Irish,
Danish, Dutch) a form
of Lucius

Lucian
(Latin) an alternate
form of Lucius

Lucius
(Latin) light, bringer
of light

Luke
(Latin) a form
of Lucius

Lyle
(French) island

Lyndon
(English)
linden-tree hill

Lynn
(English) waterfall,
brook

༄

· M ·

Mac
(Scottish) son

Macaulay
(Scottish) son of
righteousness

Mackenzie
(Irish) son of the
wise ruler

Maddox
(Welsh, English)
son of the benefactor

Magnus
(Latin) great

Maguire
(Irish) son of
the beige one

Malcolm
(Scottish) follower
of Saint Columba,
an early Scottish saint

Manuel
(Hebrew) a short form
of Emmanuel

Marcellus
(Latin) little warrior

Marcus
(Latin) martial,
warlike

Mario
(Italian)
a form of Mark

Mark
(Latin) an alternate
form of Marcus

Marshall
(French) caretaker
of the horses,
military title

Martin
(Latin) martial,
warlike

Marty
(Latin) a familiar form
of Martin

Marv
(English) a short form
of Marvin

Marvin
(English) lover
of the sea

Matt
(Hebrew) a short form
of Matthew

Matthew
(Hebrew) gift of God

Matty
(Hebrew) a familiar
form of Matthew

Maurice
(Latin) dark-skinned;
moor, marshland

Max
(Latin) a short form of
Maximilian, Maxwell

Maxfield
(English) Mack's field

Maximilian
(Latin) greatest

Maxwell
(English) great spring

Melvin
(Irish) armored chief;
(English) mill friend

Michael
(Hebrew)
who is like God?

Miles
(Greek) millstone;
(Latin) soldier

Milo
(German) an alternate
form of Miles

Milos
(Greek, Slavic)
pleasant

Milt
(English) a short form
of Milton

Milton
(English) mill town

Mitch
(English) a short form
of Mitchell

Mitchell
(English) a form of
Michael

Montgomery
(English) rich man's
mountain

Monty
(English) a familiar
form of Montgomery

Morgan
(Scottish) sea warrior

Morrie
(Latin) a familiar form
of Maurice

Morris
(Latin) dark skinned;
moor, marshland;
(English) a form of
Maurice

Mort
(French, English)
a short form of
Mortimer, Morton

Mortimer
(French) still water

Morton
(English) town near
the moor

Morven
(Scottish) mariner

Moses
(Hebrew) drawn out of
the water; (Egyptian)
son, child

Murphy
(Irish) sea-warrior

Murray
(Scottish) sailor

Myles
(Latin) soldier;
(German) an alternate
form of Miles

Myron
(Greek) fragrant oil

∽

· N ·

Nat
(English) a short form
of Nathan, Nathaniel

Nate
(Hebrew) a short form
of Nathan, Nathaniel

Nathan
(Hebrew) a short form
of Nathaniel

Nathaniel
(Hebrew) gift of God

Ned
(English) a familiar
form of Edward

Neil, Neal
(Irish) champion

Nelson
(English) son of Neil

Niall
(Irish) an alternate
form of Neil

Nicholas
(Greek) victorious
people

Nick
(English) a short form
of Nicholas

Niles
(English) son of Neil

Noah
(Hebrew) peaceful,
restful

Norbert
(Scandinavian)
brilliant hero

Norman
(French) norseman

~

· O ·

Oakley
(English)
oak-tree field

Octavius
(Latin) eighth child

Odysseus
(Greek) wrathful

Ogden
(English) oak valley

Oliver
(Latin) olive tree

Olivier
(French) a form
of Oliver

Ollie
(English) a familiar
form of Oliver

Orville
(French)
golden village

Oscar
(Scandinavian)
divine spearman

Otis
(Greek)
keen of hearing

Owen
(Irish) born to
nobility

∽

· P ·

Paddy
(Irish) a familiar form
of Patrick

Parker
(English) park keeper

Pat
(English) a short form
of Patrick

Patrick
(Latin) nobleman

Paul
(Latin) small

Paxton
(Latin) peaceful town

Percy
(French) a familiar
form of Percival

Percival
(French)
pierce the valley

Perry
(English) a familiar
form of Peter

Pete
(English) a short form
of Peter

Peter
(Greek, Latin)
small rock

Phelps
(English) son of Philip

Phil
(Greek) a short form
of Philip, Phillip

Philip, Phillip
(Greek)
lover of horses

Pierce
(English) a form
of Peter

Pierre
(French)
a form of Peter

Prescott
(English) priest's
cottage

Presley
(English) priest's
meadow

Pryor
(Latin) head of the
monastery, prior

∾

· Q ·

Quentin
(Latin) fifth;
(English) Queen's
town

Quimby
(Scandinavian)
woman's estate

Quincy
(French) fifth
son's estate

Quinlan
(Irish) strong,
well-shaped

Quinn
(Irish) a short form
of Quincy, Quinlan

∾

· R ·

Radcliff
(English) red cliff,
cliff with reeds

Radley
(English) red meadow,
meadow of reeds

Rafael
(Spanish) a form of
Raphael

Rafe
(English) a short form
of Rafferty, Ralph

Rafferty
(Irish)
prosperous, rich

Raleigh
(English) deer meadow

Ralph
(English) wolf
counselor

Ralston
(English) Ralph's
settlement

Ramsey
(English) ram's island

Rand
(English) shield;
warrior

Randall
(English) an alternate
form of Randolph

Randolph
(English) wolf with
a shield

Randy
(English) a familiar
form of Rand,
Randall, Randolph

Raphael
(Hebrew)
God has healed

Raul
(French) a form
of Ralph

Ray
(French) kingly, royal;
(English) a short form
of Rayburn, Raymond

Rayburn
(English) deer brook

Raymond
(English) mighty,
wise protector

Redmond
(English) an alternate
form of Raymond

Reece
(Welsh) enthusiastic;
stream

Reed
(English) an alternate
form of Reid

Reginald
(English) King's
advisor

Reid
(English) redheaded

Remi, Rémi
(French) alternate
form of Remy

Remington
(English) raven estate

Remy
(French) from
Rheims, France

René
(French) reborn

Reuben
(Hebrew) behold a son

Rex
(Latin) king

Reynold
(English) king's
advisor

Rhett
(Welsh) an alternate
form of Rhys

Rhys
(Welsh) an alternate
form of Reece

Rich
(English) a short form
of Richard

Richard
(English) rich and
powerful ruler

Richie
(English) a familiar
form of Richard

Richmond
(German) powerful
protector

Rick
(German) a short form
of Richard

Ricky
(English) a familiar
form of Richard, Rick

Ridley
(English) a meadow of
reeds

Rigby
(English) ruler's valley

Riley
(Irish) valiant

Riordan
(Irish) bard,
royal poet

Rip
(Dutch) ripe,
full-grown; (English)
a short form of Ripley

Ripley
(English) meadow
near the river

Roald
(Norwegian)
famous ruler

Roan
(English) a short
form of Rowan

Roarke
(Irish) famous ruler

Rob
(English) a short
form of Robert

Robbie
(English) a familiar
form of Robert

Robby
(English) a familiar
form of Robert

Robert
(English) famous
brilliance

Robin
(English) a short form
of Robert

Robinson
(English) son of
Robert

Rochester
(English) rocky
fortress

Rockwell
(English) rocky spring

Rod
(English) a short form
of Roderick, Rodney

Roddy
(English) a familiar
form of Roderick

Roderick
(German)
famous ruler

Rodger
(German) an alternate
form of Roger

Rodman
(German) famous
man, hero

Rodney
(English) island
clearing

Roger
(German) famous
spearman

Roland
(German) famous
throughout the land

Rolf
(German) a form
of Ralph

Roman
(Latin)
from Rome, Italy

Ron
(Hebrew) a short form
of Aaron, Ronald

Ronald
(Scottish) a form
of Reginald

Ronnie
(Scottish) a familiar
form of Ronald

Roosevelt
(Dutch) rose field

Rory
(German) a familiar
form of Roderick;
(Irish) red king

Roscoe
(Scandinavian)
deer forest

Ross
(Latin) rose

Rowan
(English) tree with
red berries

Roy
(French) king

Royce
(English) son of Roy

Rudolf
(German) an alternate
form of Rudolph

Rudolph
(German) famous wolf

Rudy
(English) a familiar
form of Rudolph

Rudyard
(English) red
enclosure

Rufus
(Latin) redhead

Russ
(French) a short form
of Russell

Russell
(French) redhead, fox
colored

Rusty
(French) a familiar
form of Russell

Rutherford
(English) cattle ford

Ryan
(Irish) little king

༄

· S ·

Sal
(Italian) a short
form of Salvatore

Salvatore
(Italian) savior

Sam
(Hebrew) a short
form of Samuel

Sammy
(Hebrew) a familiar
form of Samuel

Samson
(Hebrew) like the sun

Samuel
(Hebrew) heard God,
asked God

Sanford
(English)
sandy river crossing

Sargent
(French) army officer

Saul
(Hebrew) asked for,
borrowed

Sawyer
(English) wood worker

Scott
(English) from
Scotland; a familiar
form of Prescott

Seamus
(Irish) a form of James

Sean
(Irish) a form of John

Sebastian
(Greek) venerable;
(Latin) revered

Selby
(English) village by
the mansion

Seth
(Hebrew) appointed

Seymour
(French) prayer

Shane
(Irish) an alternate
form of Sean

Shannon
(Irish) small and wise

Shel
(English) a short form
of Shelby, Sheldon

Shelby
(English) ledge estate

Sheldon
(English) farm on
the ledge

Shelley
(English) a familiar
form of Shelby

Shep
(English) a short form
of Shepherd

Shepherd
(English) shepherd

Sheridan
(Irish) wild

Sherman
(English) sheep
shearer; resident of
a shire

Sherwin
(English) swift runner,
one who cuts the wind

Sherwood
(English) bright forest

Alice, Anne, Crystal, Emma, Esmé, Evelyn, Florence, Jocelyn, Kimberly, Lucy and Maud were all originally male names.

∾

Sid
(French) a short form
of Sidney

Sidney
(French) from Saint
Denis, France

Sigmund
(German) victorious
protector

Silas
(Latin) a short form
of Silvan

Silvan
(Latin) forest dweller

Silvester
(Latin) an alternate
form of Sylvester

Simon
(Hebrew) he heard

Sinclair
(French) prayer

Skip
(Scandinavian) a short
form of Skipper

Skipper
(Scandinavian)
shipmaster

Sloan
(Irish) warrior

Smith
(English) blacksmith

Solomon
(Hebrew) peaceful

Spalding
(English) divided field

Spencer
(English) dispenser
of provisions

Spenser
(English) an alternate
form of Spencer

Spiro
(Greek) round basket,
breath

Stan
(Latin, English)
a short form of Stanley

Stanford
(English) rocky ford

Stanley
(English) stony
meadow

Stephan
(Greek) an alternate
form of Stephen

Stephen
(Greek) crowned

Sterling
(English) valuable,
silver penny

Steve
(Greek) a short form
of Stephen, Steven

Steven
(Greek) crowned;
an alternate form of
Stephen

Stewart
(English) an alternate
form of Stuart

Stuart
(English) caretaker,
steward

Sullivan
(Irish) black eyed

Sully
(Irish) a familiar form
of Sullivan

Sutherland
(Scandinavian)
southern land

Sweeney
(Irish) small hero

Sy
(Latin) a short form
of Sylas

Sydney
(French) an alternate
form of Sidney

Sylas
(Latin) an alternate
form of Silas

Sylvester
(Latin) forest dweller

∾

· T ·

Tab
(German) shining,
brilliant;
(English) drummer

Tad
(Greek, Latin) a short
form of Thaddeus;
(Welsh) father

Talbot
(French) boot maker

Tate
(Scandinavian,
English) cheerful

Taylor
(English) tailor

Ted
(English) a short form
of Edward, Theodore

Teddy
(English) a familiar
form of Edward,
Theodore

Tennessee
(Cherokee) mighty
warrior

Tennyson
(English) an alternate
form of Dennison

Terrell
(German)
thunder ruler

Terrence,
Terence
(Latin) smooth

Terry
(English) a familiar
form of Terrence

Thad
(Greek, Latin) a short
form of Thaddeus

Thaddeus
(Greek) courage;
(Latin) praiser

Thatcher
(English) roof
thatcher, repairer of
roofs

Theo
(English) a short form
of Theodore

Theodore
(Greek) gift of God

Thomas
(Greek, Aramaic) twin

Thompson
(English) son of
Thomas

Thor
(Scandinavian)
thunder

Tim
(Greek) a short form
of Timothy

Timmy
(Greek) a familiar
form of Timothy

Timothy
(Greek) honoring God

Tobias
(Hebrew)
God is good

Toby
(Hebrew) a familiar
form of Tobias

Todd
(English) fox

Tom
(English) a short form
of Tomas, Thomas

Tomas
(German) a form
of Thomas

Tommie
(Hebrew) an alternate
form of Tommy

Tommy
(Hebrew) a familiar
form of Thomas

Tony
(Greek) flourishing;
(Latin) praiseworthy;
(English) a short form
of Anthony

Topher
(Greek) a short form
of Christopher

Torrence
(Latin) an alternate
form of Terrence;
(Irish) knolls

Tory
(English) a familiar
form of Torrence

Tracy
(Greek) harvester;
(Latin) courageous;
(Irish) battler

Travers
(French) crossroads

Travis
(English) a form
of Travers

Trent
(Latin) torrent,
rapid stream

Trevor
(Irish) prudent;
(Welsh) homestead

Trey
(English) three, third

Tristan
(Welsh) bold

Troy
(Irish) foot soldier;
(English) water

Truman
(English) honest

Tucker
(English) fuller,
tucker of cloth

Ty
(English) a short form
of Tyler, Tyrone

Tyler
(English) tile-maker

Tyrone
(Greek) sovereign;
(Irish) land of Owen

‿

· U ·

Ulysses
(Latin) wrathful;
a form of Odysseus

Uri
(Hebrew) a short form
of Uriah

Uriah
(Hebrew) my light

∽

· V ·

Vance
(English) marshland

Vaughn
(Welsh) small

Vern
(Latin) a short form
of Vernon

Vernon
(Latin) springlike,
youthful

Vic
(Latin) a short form
of Victor

Victor
(Latin) victor,
conqueror

Vin
(Latin) a short form
of Vincent

Vince
(English) a short form
of Vincent

Vincent
(Latin) victor,
conqueror

Vinny
(English) a familiar
form of Vincent

Virgil
(Latin) rod bearer,
staff bearer

Vito
(Latin) alive

∽

· W ·

Wainwright
(English) wagonmaker

Walker
(English) cloth walker,
cloth cleaner

Wallace
(English) form
of Wales

Wally
(English) a familiar
form of Walter

Walt
(English) a short form
of Walter, Walton

Walter
(German) army ruler,
general;
(English) woodsman

Walton
(English) walled town

Ward
(English) watchman,
guardian

Waverly
(English) quaking
aspen-tree meadow

Wayne
(English) wagonmaker;
a short form of
Wainwright

Weber
(German) weaver

Webster
(English) weaver

Wendell
(German) wanderer;
(English) good dale,
good valley

Wentworth
(English) pale man's
settlement

Wes
(English) a short form
of Wesley

Wesley
(English) western
meadow

Whit
(English) a short form
of Whitman, Whitney

Whitman
(English)
white-haired man

Whitney
(English) white island,
white water

Wilbur
(English) wall
fortification, bright
willows

Wilder
(English) wilderness,
wild

Wilfred
(German) determined
peacemaker

Wilhelm
(German) determined
guardian

Wilkie
(English) a familiar
form of Wilkins

Wilkins
(English) son of
little Will

Will
(English) a short form
of William

William
(English) determined
guardian

Willie
(German) a familiar
form of William

Willis
(German) son
of Willie

Wills
(English) son of Will

Wilmer
(German) determined
and famous

Wilt
(English) a short form
of Wilton

Wilton
(English) farm by
the spring

Winston
(English) friendly
town, victory town

Woodrow
(English) passage
in the woods

Woody
(American) a familiar
form of Woodrow

Wyatt
(French) little warrior

Wyn
(Welsh) light skinned,
white; (English) friend

∽

· X ·

Xavier
(Arabic) bright;
(Basque) owner of
the new house

Xenos
(Greek) hospitality

· Y ·

Yale
(German) productive;
(English) old

Yancy
(Native American)
Englishman, Yankee

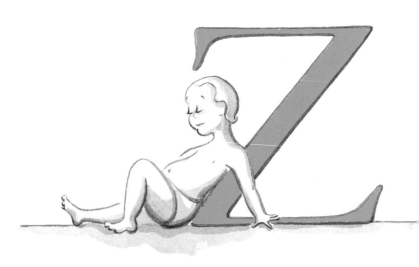

· Z ·

Zac
(Hebrew) a short form
of Zachary

Zach
(Hebrew) a short form
of Zachary

Zachary
(Hebrew)
God remembered

Zack
(Hebrew) a short form
of Zachary

Zane
(English) a form
of John

Zeke
(Hebrew) a short form
of Ezekiel, Zachary

Zeno
(Greek) cart; harness

Zeus
(Greek) living

∾

PART II

A NAME MISCELLANY

If none of the classic names seem exactly right, there are lots of other options. We've organized a selection here by category, including names from the garden, unisex names, surnames as first names and names from children's literature. Some of them could be regarded as classic, but they have a twist. They're reminiscent of a flower, a place or a favorite novel, and they're imbued with meaning beyond being just a name. This is because they call up associations like purple blossoms (Lilac) and smart school-girls (*Anne of Green Gables*).

∾

FAVORITE NAMES FROM THE GARDEN

Amaryllis	Gardenia
Angelica	Hazel
Blossom	Heather
Bryony	Holly
Camellia	Iris
Clover	Ivy
Dahlia	Jasmine
Daisy	Laurel
Fern	Liana
Flora	Lilac

Lily	Rosemary
Magnolia	Rue
Marigold	Saffron
Marguerite	Sage
Myrtle	Sequoia
Olive	Tansy
Poppy	Verbena
Posey	Violet
Petunia	Willow
Rose	

BELOVED CHARACTERS FROM CHILDREN'S LITERATURE

Ramona
Ramona the Pest
by Beverly Cleary

Wendy
Peter Pan
by J. M. Barrie

Winnie
Tuck Everlasting
by Natalie Babbitt

· B O Y S ·

Christopher
Winnie the Pooh
by A. A. Milne

Harry
*Harry Potter and the
Sorcerer's Stone*
by J. K. Rowling

Henry
Henry Huggins
by Beverly Cleary

James
James and the Giant Peach
by Roald Dahl

Jody
The Yearling
by Marjorie Kinnan
Rawlings

Leroy
Encyclopedia Brown:
Boy Detective
by Donald J. Sobol

Lyle
Lyle, Lyle, Crocodile
by Bernard Waber

Max
Where the Wild Things Are
by Maurice Sendak

Milo
The Phantom Tollbooth
by Norton Juster

Nate
Nate the Great
by Marjorie Weinnan
Sharmat

Travis
Old Yeller
by Fred Gipson

∾

SURNAMES AS FIRST NAMES

(For Boys and Girls Alike)

Ailey	Brontë
Alcott	Cabot
Beckett	Calder
Bowie	Calhoun
Branigan	Callahan
Branson	Campbell
Brennan	Carver
Brewster	Cassidy
Brody	Chan

Chandler	Dixon
Channing	Donahue
Chase	Donovan
Clayton	Duff
Cole	Dugan
Cooper	Dyson
Crosby	Edison
Dalton	Emerson
Davis	Finn
Dawson	Fitzgerald
Dempsey	Flannery
Dennison	Fletcher
Devereux	Flynn
Dix	Forrest

Fraser	Hayden
Gallagher	Hayes
Garcia	Hudson
Grady	Hunter
Griffin	Jackson
Gulliver	Jameson
Guthrie	Jenner
Hale	Keaton
Hamilton	Kennedy
Hammett	Kenyon
Hansen	Lennox
Hardy	Lincoln
Harper	Lowry
Hart	Macy

MacArthur	Murphy
Madigan	Nash
Maguire	Navarro
Mally	Oakley
Malone	O'Brien
Marley	O'Hara
Marquez	O'Keefe
Mason	Ortega
McAllister	O'Shea
McCabe	Parker
McKenzie	Paxton
Mercer	Penn
Monroe	Peyton
Morrison	Phelan

Poe	Rowan
Powell	Runyon
Presley	Ryder
Quinn	Sawyer
Raleigh	Shaw
Redmond	Sheriden
Reed	Sinclair
Remington	Slater
Reilly	Sloan
Riley	Spalding
Rockwell	Stone
Romero	Tanner
Rooney	Tate
Ross	Tennyson

Thaxter

Tucker

Tully

Twain

Tyson

Wade

Webster

Weston

Wharton

Wiley

Willoughby

Wilson

NAMES OF VIRTUE

Amity	Hope
Charity	Mercy
Chastity	Modesty
Faith	Patience
Felicity	Prudence
Fidelity	Unity
Grace	Verity
Honor	∾

The Muses

Zeus sired an extraordinary number of children, among them the Muses, his nine daughters by the Titaness Mnemosyne, the goddess of memory. Each daughter was the patroness or inspirer of a specific art, and each also has a specific attribute by which she can be identified. Today, the tragic mask of Melpomene and the comic mask of Thalia are perhaps the most familiar of these attributes.

∾

Calliope: *epic poetry*
Clio: *history*
Erato: *love poetry*

Euterpe: *lyric poetry*
Melpomene: *tragedy*
Polyhymnia: *sacred poetry*
Terpsichore: *choral song and dance*
Thalia: *comedy*
Urania: *astronomy*

PLACE NAMES

Africa	Eden
Alabama	Florence
Amarillo	Georgia
Asia	Holland
Brooklyn	India
Caledonia	Ireland
Chelsea	Lourdes
China	Madison
Dakota	Montana
	Olympia

Paris

Sahara

Savannah

Siena

Sierra

Valencia

Verona

· B O Y S ·

Austin

Cheyenne

Dallas

Denver

Dublin

Everest

Flint

Galway

Houston

Hudson

Israel

Macon

Nevada

Phoenix

Rio

Troy

York

Zaire

∽

NAMES FROM SHAKESPEARE

· GIRLS ·

Adriana
The Comedy of Errors

Beatrice
Much Ado About Nothing

Bianca
*The Taming of the Shrew;
Othello*

Cassandra
Troilus and Cressida

Cordelia
King Lear

Cressida
Troilus and Cressida

Desdemona
Othello

Diana
All's Well That Ends Well

Emilia
Othello; A Winter's Tale

Helena
*A Midsummer Night's Dream;
All's Well That Ends Well*

Imogen
Cymbeline

Isabel
Henry V

Isabella
Measure for Measure

Jessica
The Merchant of Venice

Julia
Two Gentlemen of Verona

Juliet
Romeo and Juliet

Juno
The Tempest

Lavinia
Titus Andronicus

Lucana
The Comedy of Errors

Marina
Pericles

Miranda
The Tempest

Nerissa
The Merchant of Venice

Octavia
Antony and Cleopatra

Olivia
Twelfth Night

Ophelia
Hamlet

Paulina
The Winter's Tale

Perdita
The Winter's Tale

Phebe
As You Like It

Portia
*The Merchant of Venice;
Julius Caesar*

Regan
King Lear

Rosalind
As You Like It

Rosaline
Love's Labour's Lost

Tamora
Titus Andronicus

Titania
A Midsummer Night's Dream

Viola
Twelfth Night

· B O Y S ·

Adrian
The Tempest

Alonso
The Tempest

Angus
Macbeth

Antonio
*The Tempest; Two Gentleman
of Verona; The Merchant of
Venice; Much Ado About
Nothing*

Balthasar
*Romeo and Juliet; The
Merchant of Venice; Much
Ado About Nothing*

Claudio
*Measure for Measure; Much
Ado About Nothing*

Cornelius
Hamlet

Dion
The Winter's Tale

Duncan
Macbeth

Fabian
Twelfth Night

Francisco
Hamlet

Gregory
Romeo and Juliet

Horatio
Hamlet

Humphrey
Henry VI, Part II

Lorenzo
The Merchant of Venice

Lucius
*Timon of Athens; Titus
Andronicus; Julius Caesar*

Malcolm
Macbeth

Oliver
As You Like It

Orlando
As You Like It

Owen
Henry IV, Part I

Philo
Antony and Cleopatra

Sampson
Romeo and Juliet

Sebastian
Twelfth Night; The Tempest

Timon
Measure for Measure

Toby
Twelfth Night

∾

Charles Dickens named his seven sons after famous literary figures. Their names were Alfred Tennyson Dickens; Francis Jeffrey Dickens; Henry Fielding Dickens; Sydney Smith Haldimand Dickens; Walter Landor Dickens; Edward Bulwer Lytton Dickens; and (after himself) Charles Culliford Boz Dickens. He almost immediately gave each son a nickname.

ROYAL FAVORITES

*(From the British, Scottish,
and European Royal Families)*

· GIRLS ·

Adela

Adelaide

Agnes

Alberta

Alexandra

Alice

Amelia

Anne

Arabella

Augusta

Beatrice

Birgitte

Camille

Caroline

Catherine

Charlotte

Christina

Claudine

Constance

Dorothea	Isabel
Edith	Isabella
Eleanor	Jane
Elizabeth	Joan
Ella	Julia
Emma	Juliana
Eugenie	Louisa
Feodora	Louise
Gabriella	Lucy
Gertrude	Margaret
Grace	Marina
Helen	Mary
Helena	Matilda
Henrietta	Maud

	·BOYS·
May	Albert
Olga	Alexander
Olivia	Alfred
Pauline	Andrew
Philippa	Antony
Rose	Arthur
Sarah	Charles
Sophia	Christian
Stephanie	Constantine
Victoria	Duff
Wilhelmina	Duncan
Zara	Edgar
	Edward

Edmund	Louis
Ernest	Michael
Finlay	Nicholas
Francis	Patrick
Franklin	Paul
Frederick	Peter
George	Philip
Harold	Richard
Harry	Stephen
Henry	Thomas
Hugh	Victor
James	Walter
John	William
Leopold	∾

PART III

THE
MOST POPULAR NAMES
OF THE
TWENTIETH CENTURY
(AND INTO THE TWENTY-FIRST)

Names that were popular in the early 1900s may seem old-fashioned, but they are coming back in strength. Mothers lately have been joking that the kids in their play groups sound more like a bunch of convalescing seniors than infants—Max, Lily, Gus, Ruth and Sophie. There's a reason why these names are making a comeback. They remind us of a simpler time, and maybe even of beloved grandmothers and grandfathers. These lists arranged by decade may remind you of family names, or give you ideas for names that are linked with eras you admire.

∽

The Ten Most Popular Names
of the 1900s

· GIRLS ·	· BOYS ·
Mary	John
Helen	William
Margaret	James
Anna	George
Ruth	Joseph
Elizabeth	Charles
Dorothy	Robert
Marie	Frank
Mildred	Edward
Alice	Henry

The Ten Most Popular Names
of the 1910s

· G I R L S ·	· B O Y S ·
Mary	John
Helen	William
Dorothy	James
Margaret	Robert
Ruth	Joseph
Mildred	George
Anna	Charles
Elizabeth	Edward
Frances	Frank
Marie	Walter

The Ten Most Popular Names of the 1920s

· G I R L S ·	· B O Y S ·
Mary	Robert
Dorothy	John
Helen	James
Betty	William
Margaret	Charles
Ruth	George
Virginia	Joseph
Doris	Richard
Mildred	Edward
Elizabeth	Donald

The Ten Most Popular Names of the 1930s

· GIRLS ·	· BOYS ·
Mary	Robert
Betty	James
Barbara	John
Shirley	William
Patricia	Richard
Dorothy	Charles
Joan	Donald
Margaret	George
Nancy	Thomas
Helen	Joseph

The Ten Most Popular Names of the 1940s

·GIRLS·	·BOYS·
Mary	James
Linda	Robert
Barbara	John
Patricia	William
Carol	Richard
Sandra	David
Nancy	Charles
Judith	Thomas
Sharon	Michael
Susan	Ronald

The Ten Most Popular Names of the 1950s

·GIRLS·	·BOYS·
Mary	Michael
Linda	James
Patricia	Robert
Susan	John
Deborah	David
Barbara	William
Debra	Richard
Karen	Thomas
Nancy	Mark
Donna	Charles

The Ten Most Popular Names
of the 1960s

·GIRLS·	·BOYS·
Lisa	Michael
Mary	David
Karen	John
Susan	James
Kimberly	Robert
Patricia	Mark
Linda	William
Donna	Richard
Michelle	Thomas
Cynthia	Jeffrey

The Ten Most Popular Names of the 1970s

·GIRLS·	·BOYS·
Jennifer	Michael
Amy	Christopher
Melissa	Jason
Michelle	David
Kimberly	James
Lisa	John
Angela	Robert
Heather	Brian
Stephanie	William
Jessica	Matthew

The Ten Most Popular Names of the 1980s

·GIRLS·	·BOYS·
Jessica	Michael
Jennifer	Christopher
Amanda	Matthew
Ashley	Joshua
Sarah	David
Stephanie	Daniel
Melissa	James
Nicole	Robert
Elizabeth	John
Heather	Joseph

The Ten Most Popular Names of the 1990s

· G I R L S ·	· B O Y S ·
Ashley	Michael
Jessica	Christopher
Emily	Matthew
Sarah	Joshua
Samantha	Jacob
Brittany	Andrew
Amanda	Daniel
Elizabeth	Nicholas
Taylor	Tyler
Megan	Joseph

The Ten Most Popular Names
in 2000

· G I R L S ·	· B O Y S ·
Emily	Jacob
Hannah	Michael
Madison	Matthew
Ashley	Joshua
Sarah	Christopher
Alexis	Nicholas
Samantha	Andrew
Jessica	Joseph
Taylor	Daniel
Elizabeth	Tyler

The Ten Most Popular Names
in 2001

·GIRLS·	·BOYS·
Emily	Jacob
Madison	Michael
Hannah	Matthew
Ashley	Joshua
Alexis	Christopher
Samantha	Nicholas
Sarah	Andrew
Abigail	Joseph
Elizabeth	Daniel
Jessica	William

The Ten Most Popular Names in 2002

·GIRLS·	·BOYS·
Emily	Jacob
Madison	Michael
Hannah	Joshua
Emma	Matthew
Alexis	Ethan
Ashley	Joseph
Abigail	Andrew
Sarah	Christopher
Samantha	Daniel
Olivia	Nicholas

The Ten Most Popular Names in 2003

· GIRLS ·	· BOYS ·
Emily	Jacob
Emma	Michael
Madison	Joshua
Hannah	Matthew
Olivia	Andrew
Abigail	Joseph
Alexis	Ethan
Ashley	Daniel
Elizabeth	Christopher
Samantha	Anthony

· PART IV ·

NICKNAMES

Did you have a nickname growing up? It's one of those inevitable first-date questions along with "Do you have any siblings?" and "Where are you from?" You want your son or daughter to enjoy this friendly appellation, so be sure his nickname is a good one. Those that follow aren't the types of nicknames that come from shortening a first name. They're the nicknames bestowed by life, when a younger sibling can't pronounce his brother's first name, or when a child shows a real predilection for a certain type of food. Peaches, for example, or Twinkie.

෴

·BOYS·

Ace	Governor
Biff	Lefty
Bud	Mack
Buster	Moodoggie
Butch	Pops
Buzz	Red
Champ	Slim
Chief	Scooter
Chip	Skippy
Chopper	Smitty
Dash	Speedy
Digger	Spike
Dutch	Sport
	Stretch

· G I R L S ·

Babe	Mitzie
Baby	Muffy
Birdy	Pebbles
Bitsy	Pet
Bubbles	Pinky
Buffy	Red
Bunny	Rusty
Buzzy	Short Stack
Cookie	Spike
Happy	Sunshine
Half Pint	Tiny
Lucky	Tootsie
	Trixie

[235]

BIBLIOGRAPHY

Hamlin, Grace. *The Penguin Classic Baby Name Book: 2,000 Names from the World's Great Literature*. New York, New York: Penguin USA, 2001.

Lansky, Bruce. *The Very Best Baby Name Book in the Whole World*. Rev. ed. Minnetonka, Minnesota: Meadowbrook Press, 1995.

Lipson, Eden Ross. *The New York Times Guide to the Best Books for Children*. Revised and Updated. New York, New York: Times Books, 1988, 1991.

Orenstein, Peggy. "Where Have All the Lisas Gone?" *The New York Times Magazine* (July 6, 2003): 28–31.

Rosenkrantz, Linda and Pamela Redmond Satran. *Beyond Jennifer & Jason, Madison & Montana*. New York, New York: St. Martin's Paperbacks, 2000.

Rosenkrantz, Linda and Pamela Redmond Satran. *An Anglophile's Guide to Baby Naming*. New York, New York: St. Martin's Press, 1992.

Silverstein, Alvin, Virginia, Robert, Linda, Laura, and Kevin. *John, Your Name is Famous: Highlights, Anecdotes & Trivia About the Name John and the People Who Made It Great*. Lebanon, New Jersey: Avstar Publishing Corp., 1989.

Stafford, Diane. *40,001 Best Baby Names*. Naperville, Illinois: Sourcebooks, Inc., 2003.

Wallace, Carol McD. *20,001 Names for Baby*. New York, New York: Quill, 1995.

INDEX

G

Gabriel, 140
Gabriela, Gabriella, 52, 213
Gabrielle, 52
Gaby, 52
Gail, 52
Gallagher, 140, 197
Galway, 206
Garcia, 197
Gardenia, 190
garden-related names, 190–191
Gardner, 140
Gareth, 140
Garrett, 140
Garth, 140
Gary, 140
Gay, 52
Gayle, 52
Geena, 52
Gene, 140
Generosa, 52
Genevieve, 52
Geoff, 140
Geoffrey, 140
George, 140, 215, 218, 219, 220, 221
Georgeanne, 52
Georgene, 52
Georgette, 52
Georgia, 53, 204
Georgianna, 53
Georgina, 53
Gerald, 140
Geraldine, 53
Gerard, 140
Geri, 53
Germaine, 53
Gerry, 140
Gertrude, 53, 213

Gideon, 141
Gifford, 141
Gigi, 53
Gilbert, 141
Gilberte, 53
Gilda, 53
Gillian, 53
Gina, 53
Ginger, 54
Ginny, 54
Giovanni, 150
girl names. *See also*
    popular names;
    specific names
    boy names
        becoming,
        18, 173
    children's-
        literature-
        related names,
        192–193
    nicknames,
        233, 235
    place names,
        204–205
    uniqueness of,
        12–13
Giselle, 54
Gladys, 54
Glen, Glenn, 141
Glenda, 54
Glendon, 141
Glenna, 54
Gloria, 54
Glory, 54
Glynnis, 54
Godfrey, 141
Golda, 54
Gordon, 141
Governor, 234
Grace, 54, 201, 213

Grady, 141, 197
Graham, 141
Granger, 141
Grant, 141
Grantland, 141
Granville, 141
Gray, 141
Graydon, 141
Grayson, 142
Greer, 54
Greg, Gregg, 142
Gregory, 142, 210
Greta, 54
Gretchen, 55
Griffin, 142, 197
Griffith, 142
Griselda, 55
Guinevere, 55
Gulliver, 197
Gus, 142
Gussie, 55
Gustave, 142
Guthrie, 197
Guy, 142
Gwen, 55
Gwendolyn, 55
Gwyneth, 55

H

Hadassah, 56
Hadley, 56, 143
Hailey, 56
Hal, 143
Hale, 197
Haley, 56, 143
Half Pint, 235
Hall, 143
Hallie, 56
Hamilton, 143, 197
Hammett, 197